Magnificent Monuments of India

Taj Mahal

The Story of a Wonder of the World

Tilottama Shome

Illustrated by Kavita Singh Kale

talking
CUB

An Imprint of Speaking Tiger Books

TALKING CUB

125A, Ground Floor, Shahpur Jat,
Near Asiad Village, New Delhi - 110 049

First published in paperback in Talking Cub
by Speaking Tiger Books in 2021

Book design by Maithili Doshi Aphale

ISBN: 978-93-5447-247-3

eISBN: 978-93-5447-246-6

10 9 8 7 6 5 4 3 2 1

*To Ma and Baba, for an early start into
the world of forts and castles.
To Pranay, for a supportive fascination of history-geography.
To Pia and Sophie, for being experts who can distinguish between
the stench of bat poo and rancid mold.*

Contents

An Emperor Without a Throne

Shah Jahan sat at his window. His daughter Jahanara was at his feet, reading out loud from Babur's journals—like she had been doing for years. The Mughal emperor was old now, and tired. He often wanted to hear the words of his great-grandfather Babur, recorded in his autobiography *Baburnama*. And he also wanted to gaze at the morning mist rising from the Yamuna river that was flowing outside the fort. The mist slightly obscured the Taj Mahal, on the opposite bank, giving it a magical appearance.

Shah Jahan was now an emperor in captivity, held in the Agra Fort by his son Aurangzeb, with his eldest daughter his only companion. Spending his days remembering his past, the Taj Mahal across the river from his prison reminded him of his glory days.

He thought often of his beloved Mumtaz Mahal, whom he had married in 1612. Until her death in 1631, they had

remained constant companions. Those days made for such happy memories.

Visions of their royal engagement ceremony came to his mind. In 1607, at the fort of Lahore, in the presence of his father Jahangir, he had placed the 'ring of luck' on the finger of Mumtaz Mahal, who was then known as Arjumand Banu Begum .

He could see Mumtaz Mahal sitting atop a bejewelled elephant, inside a curtained howdah, as the Mughal army marched across the Deccan plains. She was always by his side through all his military campaigns across Hindustan. As he, then called Shah Khurram, travelled from Rajasthan to the Deccan kingdoms, conducting campaigns to annex more and more land for Emperor Jahangir, Mumtaz Mahal raised his children and ran his household from the zenana which moved with him.

On the day he became the emperor—Padshah—at the Agra Fort, in 1628, Mumtaz Mahal had been the first one in the zenana to congratulate him by scattering gems and rubies over his head.

But that joy was short-lived, and in 1631, Mumtaz died, after giving birth to a little girl. Shah Jahan looked at his daughter Jahanara, sitting across him, and remembered her weeping over the dead body of her mother. They were in the palace in Burhanpur, and the newly born Gauhara was wailing pitifully in the arms of the nurse. She was their fourteenth child.

For two years after Mumtaz's death, Shah Jahan was in deep mourning. He gave up listening to music, and wore only white clothes. His eyes got affected from constant weeping and he needed spectacles. Later, someone would record that his beard turned 'grey, and eventually white'.

This was when he decided to build a grand mausoleum in the memory of his beloved Mumtaz Mahal. Even in his sorrow he knew that this would be his grandest project yet—a tomb or maqbara of such beauty that no one in the world had seen before.

He imagined this wondrous building at the bend of a mighty river—one of the many Himalayan snow-fed rivers that flowed through the northern plains of Hindustan. Where would such a place be? The Mughal Empire at that time was at its largest, spread over the subcontinent. But only one city came to the emperor's mind. The mighty city of Agra, where his ancestors had spent years building forts, gardens, palaces and tombs. It was next to the river Yamuna that irrigated the plains. He could imagine his wife's grave entombed in a beautiful building next to the river amidst lush gardens. It would be as though she was laying in Paradise, as he had read it described in the holy books.

And so Agra it was, the city chosen to house what would one day be a wonder of the world—the Taj Mahal.

The city of Agra was made famous by the Mughal kings. But it has a history that predates them. Agra existed 2500 years ago! Archaeological digs have unearthed pottery in the area that date back to 1800 BCE. In fact, the region of Agravan is mentioned in the epic Mahabahrata, so its origins go back to mythical times. It is said that Krishna lived in the neighbouring villages of Mathura and Vrindavan at various times of his life. There are versions of Agra's history that claim that it was founded by Agrasen, Krishna's maternal grandfather, and probably started as a cluster of huts surrounded by fields. At that time, Mathura was the more prosperous town and Agra was a small outpost of the Surasena dynasty to which Krishna belonged.

The Greek geographer and Alexander's general Ptolemy was the first person to mark Agra with that name on a map. He had travelled to the region around 323-283 BCE. The city continued to exist under various rulers. The Lodi dynasty took over the city in the early 15th century. Illustrious rulers like Sikander Lodi and Ibrahim Lodi ruled it till the Mughals swept them aside.

Babur, the first Mughal to rule in Hindustan, made Agra one of the most prosperous cities of the world, often compared to London, Paris and Constantinople. Babur had travelled from Persia and entered Hindustan from Kabul, and he was nostalgic for the gardens and running waters of Kabul. He hated the heat and dust of Agra. And so he started building the first geometric gardens here, where he could have shade-giving trees and bath houses and cool pavilions with water wheels that would bring up water from the Yamuna.

As the Mughal dynasty continued to rule under Humayun, Akbar and Jahangir, the city of Agra flourished. A melting pot

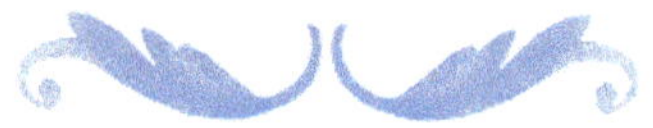

Father Montserrate, a Portugese priest, who kept records of Akbar's court wrote about Agra: 'All the necessities of human life can be obtained here if desired. This is even true of articles which have to be imported from distant corners of Europe.'

of merchants, travellers and craftsmen from all over the world, Agra was a famous destination to visit.

So Agra, with the majestic Agra Fort, beautiful riverfront gardens overlooking the Yamuna, and a thriving population, became Shah Jahan's choice as the perfect location for building the Taj Mahal.

The story of the Taj Mahal is as much about art and beauty, as it is about the times in which it was built. Today, it has become a symbol of love, but along with that it is the pinnacle of an empire's achievement. It symbolizes the might and far-reaching influence of the Mughals in the history and culture of India. Shah Jahan's biographer, Abd-al-Hamid Lahawari wrote that the Taj Mahal will be 'a memorial to the sky-reaching ambition of His Majesty… and its strength will represent the firmness of the intentions of its builder.'

The Taj Mahal is now counted amongst the New Seven Wonders of the World. It was certainly built with posterity in mind. In the words of another historian of Shah Jahan, Qazwini, the building would be 'a masterpiece for ages to come'.

But before we see the Taj Mahal and understand how it was built, let us first wander back a hundred years before it was built and see how the Great Mughals—Shah Jahan's forefathers—arrived in Hindustan and how they shaped the history and culture of the subcontinent.

Who Were the Mughals?

The Mughals ruled in India for over three hundred years. At the time when the empire was at its largest, it extended from Kabul in Afghanistan in the west to Bengal in the east.

The founder of the Mughal dynasty in India was Babur, who ruled from 1526-1530, after he defeated the Lodi dynasty of the Delhi Sultanate. He travelled to India from Samarqand (in modern Uzbekistan) and was a descendant of Timur from his father's side and of Genghis Khan on his mother's side.

Babur was a great adventurer and ruler. He wrote *Baburnama*, his autobiography, in which he described his campaigns in Central Asia and India. Detailed descriptions of life in encampments as he travelled from place to place, notes on the flora and fauna of Hindustan and his thoughts and philosophy make the *Baburnama* a remarkable document of the times.

In it, he also set down the ideal qualities of a ruler—education, truthfulness, humanity and dignity. The *Baburnama* became a foundation book of the Mughal dynasty, though in the later years, many of these qualities became diluted as the power of the empire grew.

Babur was succeeded by his son Humayun in 1530. However, in 1543, Humayun was defeated by Sher Shah and had to flee to Iran where he lived as a guest of the ruler for twelve years.

A King in Exile

Humayun had fled to Persia with his wife Hamida Banu, abandoning his kingdom. His son Akbar was left in the care of his 'milk mothers'—Maham Anaga and Jiji Anaga and Bega Begum, one of Humayun's wives.

The royal party that fled was a small group of thirty people, making their way through treacherous, cold mountains. It was a difficult journey for the group, travelling through intense cold and inhospitable conditions. Food was scarce and there are accounts of a horse from the royal party being killed and its flesh boiled in a helmet and eaten.

In Persia, Humayun and his entourage were welcomed by the Shah of Persia, Shah Tahmasp. He gave a royal decree that the visitor and his family be welcomed as visiting royalty. No effort was spared to make the Mughals comfortable. For the travellers, who had arrived through terrible conditions, the luxuries extended to them were almost unbelievable. After wandering hungry and cold through desert lands, they were now being plied with cooling sherbets and delicious banquets of hundreds of dishes. The Persians took it upon themselves to make Humayun and his entourage honoured guests. It was the beginning of a long period of Persian influences on the Mughals.

During their period of exile, Humayun and Hamida travelled through the cities of Persia and everywhere they went they were hosted magnificently. Later, when Humayun met the Shah at the latter's summer palace in the mountains, the Shah insisted that his Mughal guest convert from Sunni to Shi'ite, an alternative form of Islam that Shah Tahmasp had introduced in Persia. Humayun did not fuss about this too much as he was well aware that the hospitality of the Shah would be affected by his reaction.

There were many cultural exchanges between the Mughals and the Persians during Humayun's period of exile. Shah Tahmasp was himself an accomplished painter and a patron of artists, historians and poets. Humayun and Hamida Banu, during their travels in Persia, were able to appreciate the fine nuances of Persian art and culture which was at its zenith of sophistication at that time. While enjoying the hospitality of their hosts, they also got to taste the local cuisine.

When Humayun left Persia to return and re-conquer Hindustan, he brought back Persian influences in food, cavalry, and the arts. But the most valuable influence brought back by Humayun was something that changed the face of Indian art of the times. By this time, Tahmasp had become tired of painting and allowed two of his young

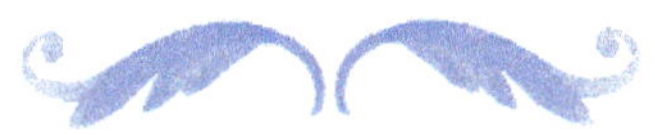

At Humayun's farewell banquet, the Shah requested a **Hindustani banquet.** Amongst the many delicious dishes cooked by the Hindustanis, the khichdi cooked with large quantities of ghee was new to the Persians. Ghee and turmeric were new ingredients that the Hindustanis introduced into the kitchens of their hosts.

artists, Mir Sayyid Ali and Abd Al-Samad to leave for Humayun's court. Under Humayun, and later under Akbar's patronage, the Persian influence became the basic element of Mughal miniature painting.

It took Humayun ten years—from 1545 to 1555—to finally march back into Hindustan via Kabul after defeating his brothers and Sher Shah. The thirteen-year-old Akbar accompanied him back to Delhi. But within six months of this, Humayun died, falling down a flight of stairs at his library, while trying to bend in prayer. Akbar succeeded him as Padshah Ghazi in 1556 and went on to become the greatest of the Great Mughals, ruling till his death in 1605.

A Mighty Emperor

Akbar expanded the Mughal Empire to cover most of India. He recaptured Kabul and Kandahar in Afghanistan and brought back the north-west frontier within the Mughal borders. He was a great administrator and an inclusive ruler. Under him, the Muslims, Hindus, Turks, Afghans and Iranians together formed the nobility and the ruling class of India.

He was tolerant of all religions, which made him unique amongst the rulers in Asia at that time. Akbar was also a prolific builder. He built forts, mosques and residences all over the country, his style of architecture being a fusion of regional Indian style and Central Asian influences. The use of red sandstone along with white marble became a signature style of Akbari architecture.

During his rule, Bega Begum, one of the widows of Humayun, and Akbar's stepmother, moved to Delhi. She had been left behind in Kabul when Humayun had fled to Persia. At that time, she had helped raise Akbar and was very fond of him. Akbar told Abul Fazl, his historian, 'the kindness and affection she showed me and my love for her are beyond expression'. He also said that people who did not know that she was a stepmother assumed that she was his mother.

After Humayun's death, Bega Begum decided to remain in Delhi where her late husband was interred. One of the first Mughal women to travel to Mecca on a Haj pilgrimage, she came back from there with masons and scholars.

After settling in Delhi, she began the work to build a grand mausoleum for Humayun's grave for which she engaged a Persian craftsman, Mirak Mirza Ghiyas, as the chief architect. The tomb became the first structure by the Mughals in Hindustan that combined certain Central Asian influences like the Timurid onion dome, and a symmetrical plan with the tomb at the centre of a charbagh. The charbagh was a symmetrical garden with water channels. It was supposed to depict Paradise, where the virtuous went after death. This was combined with Hindustani elements of local red sandstone

◆ *Humayun's Tomb*

and white marble. The garden was laid with local flowering shrubs.

Humayun's Tomb, as this mausoleum went on to be called, is a graceful and dignified structure that still stands in the heart of Delhi. Here we can see how Persian and Indian sensibilities came together, and how it foreshadows the design of the Taj Mahal.

Enter, an Unforgettable Empress

When Akbar died, he left a united Mughal Empire with a strong administrative base. He was succeeded by his son Jahangir, who, besides being an able ruler, had many other achievements. He wrote his memoirs in great detail and was an expert naturalist. His study of the breeding habits of the sarus crane was considered original research in the field of ornithology. He also encouraged and developed Mughal miniature paintings, bringing in European influences. His design of Akbar's tomb in Sikandra was a highlight of the architecture of his times. His love for nature led him to design the beautiful Mughal gardens in Srinagar, where he spent the summer months, moving there with the royal family and his court officials.

Jahangir's principal wives were Rajput royalty from whom he had various children. But in 1611, during the annual Navroz festivities, an eighteen-day spring festival originally celebrated by the Persians and later revived in Hindustan by Akbar, Jahangir met Mehr-un-Nisa. She was of Persian descent and

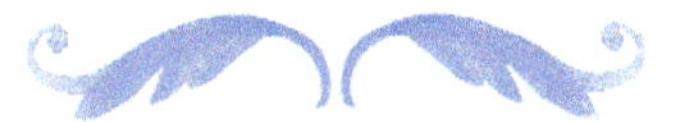

Jahangir appreciated **art and beauty** in many forms. He was extremely fond of jewellery and fashionable clothing. His knowledge of gem and jewellery was deep and he wore different jewellery everyday. He started the trend of decorating turbans with miniature paintings—a unique form of decoration compared to the earlier form where gems and jewellery were used to decorate the headgear of the nobility.

the widowed daughter of one of his nobles, Mirza Ghiyas Beg. In the meena bazaar set up at the festival, amongst the beautifully decorated shamianas, the royal ladies were allowed to meet the emperor without their veils. This is where Jahangir saw Meher-un-Nisa and fell in love with her beauty and grace. He married her within two months and she was given the title Noor Jahan, 'Light of the World'. She soon became the most influential wife of Jahangir.

Within a few years of this marriage, Jahangir's reign was mostly controlled by Noor Jahan. She was an able administrator and her position as the principal queen of the Padshah was established when she became one of the few women for whom drums were beaten in advance, before her arrival.

Thomas Roe, the first official English ambassador to the Mughal court, noted in his records, with surprise, that in Jahangir's court, women such as Noor Jahan owned ships and conducted successful international trade. She often sat behind the screens during court proceedings and addressed the Padshah directly, which was unusual for the Mughal noblewomen. Through her various business ventures, Noor Jahan accumulated enough personal wealth to construct buildings, sponsor charity and give lavish gifts. She organized a weighing ceremony of Jahangir on his birthday in 1621 where she gave gifts of jewellery, horses, elephants, beautiful dresses and trays of money to the Padshah's servants and staff. Her father was given the title of Itmad-ud-Daulah, and after he passed away, Jahangir made her the heir of his estate. This made her one of the wealthiest women in the Mughal empire, maybe even the world.

With her wealth, Noor Jahan constructed many exceptionally designed buildings. She built a huge caravanserai outside Agra called Serai Noor Mahal, which could accommodate two thousand travellers and their camels and horses. And unlike other caravensaerais of the time, which were made of brick, this one was made of red sandstone brought from Fatehpur Sikri and was richly decorated. After her parents' death—they died within a few months of each other—she started work on constructing a tomb for them in Agra. This structure stands as an example of exquisite craftsmanship. The design and craftsmanship were a confluence of Persian, Mughal and Hindustani elements. It was the first Mughal tomb that was built in white marble, instead of red sandstone. Detailed inlay work covers the mausoleum. The floors have beautiful geometric patterns. Richly decorated screens (jaalis) let in light and air. Noor Jahan's tribute to her parents was as precious and delicate as the jewellery she adored, and it went on to be a stepping stone to the artwork at the Taj Mahal.

In his later years, Jahangir suffered from ill health for prolonged periods. Noor Jahan looked after him and took over several aspects of running the empire. The influence of her family also grew over the years. While her father had risen to the prime ministership of the empire before he died, her brother Asaf Khan was an influential nobleman as well. During the course of interactions between these two families, Asaf Khan's daughter, Arjumand Banu Begum, was married to Jahangir's third son, Prince Khurram. He was later to become Shah Jahan.

When Jahangir died, Shah Jahan became the emperor after killing his brothers. You can see how Babur's values of a ruler had greatly diminished by then with brother killing brother for the crown. With his ascension, Noor Jahan also lost all her powers. She was shorn of all authority and was sent to live the rest of her life in Lahore in relative obscurity. But between her and her husband Jahangir, they left behind a legacy that was rich in artistic evolution.

Shah Jahan and Arjumand Begum moved to Agra as the new reigning couple. The queen was renamed Mumtaz Mahal. However, her years as the the Padshah Begum would be shortlived, and her death would sow the seeds of an idea of a magnificent tribute, that would go on to become the beautiful Taj Mahal.

The Emperor Who Lost His Queen

Baba Khurram, as Shah Jahan was fondly called by his father Jahangir, was the emperor's third son, after Khusrau and Parwiz. He was named Khurram by his grandfather, Akbar, which meant Joyous.

Khurram's mother was a Rajput princess from Jodhpur, Jagat Gosain. The practice of the Mughals marrying into illustrious Indian ruling families, irrespective of religious or cultural differences, was started by Akbar. This allowed the Mughal empire to gain sovereignty over these states while allowing their rulers some autonomy. It was one of the ways the Mughal Empire expanded in Hindustan. Jahangir himself was the son of a Rajput princess from Amber. This made Shah Jahan three-quarters Rajput Hindu by lineage!

Akbar instructed that Khurram be brought up by one of his own wives, Ruqaiya Sultan Begum who did not have any children. The prince grew up speaking Persian and Hindi, but did not pick up Turki which was the language that the Mughals originally spoke. Several distinguished scholars and warriors looked after his education. Khurram became an accomplished swordsman and marksman. He enjoyed the sport of hunting and shooting so much that in later years he would even give names to his favourite guns!

Khurram soon distinguished himself as the most promising prince of the family and by the time he was fifteen, in 1607, he was given his first military rank and the right to use a red tent in military camp—a privilege given to the eldest son.

In the same year, Khurram was engaged to Arjumand Banu Begum, the fourteen-year-old granddaughter of Ghiyas Beg, an important Persian nobleman of the Mughal court.

A Nobleman in Jahangir's Court

The journey of Ghiyas Beg was interesting. He came to Hindustan in 1576, from

♦ *Emperor Shah Jahan on the Peacock Throne*

Isfahan in Persia, looking for better career prospects. Akbar was known to welcome foreigners to his court. So this became an obvious destination. Also, while the Mughals, being Shia Muslims were suspicious of the Sunni Persians, they welcomed the latter for their rich cultural and artistic traditions. This was a mindset that had been established at the time of Humayun's rule, thanks to his extensive wanderings in Persia while in exile.

Ghiyas Beg travelled to India on a caravan route with his wife and three children. His wife was pregnant at the time and gave birth to their daughter Mehr-un-Nisa during the journey, in Kandahar. Beg presented himself at Akbar's court in Fatehpur Sikri and was soon appointed as revenue minister in Kabul. As he worked his way through the years, he was rewarded with a senior position in Jahangir's administration and went on to earn himself the title of Itmad-ud-Daulah, or Pillar of the State. His son Asaf Khan also got a position in the court of Jahangir and later became a pivotal character in court intrigues and in Shah Jahan's ascension to the throne. It was Asaf Khan's daughter, Arjumand Banu, who was engaged to the young Khurram in 1607, in a glittering ceremony in the zenana of the Lahore fort.

However, after the engagement, for reasons that are not clearly known, Arjumand Banu and Khurram were not married for five years. During this prolonged period of waiting, Khurram was married to a descendant of the Shah of Persia. It is believed that this was a political alliance.

◆ *Shah Jahan and Mumtaz Mahal*

In the same year as the engagement, Itmad-ud-Daulah's daughter, Mehr-un-Nisa, who also happened to be Arjumand Banu's aunt, came to live in the imperial zenana. She had been married at seventeen to Sher Afghan, a Persian mercenary who worked in the Mughal army under Jahangir. During the last years of Akbar's reign, when Jahangir was consolidating his power as heir to the throne, Sher Afghan remained loyal to Akbar and hence was seen as a potential rebel by Jahangir. After the new Padshah Jahangir took over, Sher Afghan was sent to a distant posting in Bengal. There, during an official visit by the governor, he was assassinated.

Meher-un-Nisa, now thirty and widowed, was sent to Jahangir's zenana in Agra as a lady-in-waiting to one of Akbar's dowager queens. This was part of Mughal tradition where the widows and surviving family members of officials were given shelter and positions of dignity in the imperial household.

As we read earlier, within a few years of Mehr-un-Nisa moving to Agra, she met Jahangir. The emperor fell in love with her beauty and grace and soon married her. She became Jahangir's twentieth and last wife. Renamed Noor Jahan by her husband, within six months of her marriage she became a powerful force in the Mughal empire.

With her aunt at the helm, Arjumand Banu's marriage was soon solemnized with Sultan Khurram in 1612. Amidst great fanfare and pomp, the emperor presided over the ceremony and further strengthened the ties between these two families.

The Chosen One of the Palace

Sultan Khurram was enamoured by his beautiful wife and named her Mumtaz Mahal or the Chosen One of the Palace. While he had two more wives—he had a third marriage later—Mumtaz Mahal remained his favourite partner. His biographer, Qazwini wrote, 'And always that Lady of the Age was the companion, close confidante, associate and intimate friend of that successful ruler, in hardship and comfort, joy and grief, when travelling or in residence.'

By 1617, Khurram had been given the title of Shah Jahan, King of the World, by his father Jahangir. He was the heir apparent and Jahangir entrusted him with all major military campaigns. One of his early assignments took him to

Rajasthan. His entourage, including the zenana and Mumtaz Mahal, moved with him to the Ajmer Fort. In the next four years she gave birth to four children, in Ajmer. The eldest of these children was her daughter Jahanara Begum, who would go on to be an important part of the ruling family. Her fourth child was a son, Shah Shuja.

Jahangir was extremely fond of all his grandchildren, but especially of Shah Shuja. The child suffered from infantile epilepsy and his seizures traumatized Jahangir. Shah Shuja was treated in many ways but when all failed, Jahangir took a vow that he would not harm any living thing with his own hands. He kept his promise and stopped hunting. After a few years when the child had a particularly bad fit of epilepsy and his life was in danger, Jahangir consulted an astrologer who assured him that the young boy would survive, but in his place another child would die. In a bizarre coincidence, Shah Shuja recovered from his disease and Khurram's child from his third marriage died around the same time, making the prophecy come true.

In 1616, the Sultans of Deccan became a menacing problem to the Mughals and Shah Jahan moved with his troops and family to Burhanpur, Madhya Pradesh, to quell the Sultans. Mumtaz Mahal set up her home in the Badshahi Qila. Roshanara, a daughter, was born in 1617 and a son, Aurangzeb, was born while she was travelling from Gujarat to Ujjain, yet again accompanying her husband while pregnant, on one of his postings.

Shah Jahan had been readying himself to be the heir to Jahangir. The emperor however was fully under the control of Noor Jahan and she was reluctant to back Shah Jahan as the heir. She feared a loss of her own power if he were to become king. Over the later years, as Jahangir moved to Kashmir with his court, in a bid to improve his failing health, Noor Jahan transferred her loyalties to Khusrau, Jahangir's other son. This made Shah Jahan wary of his stepmother's political ambitions. When the Sultans of Deccan attacked the Mughal forces again in Burhanpur and Jahangir asked Shah Jahan to go there to defend themselves, he decided to take Khusrau with him as insurance against possible political sabotage.

Noor Jahan continued her political games and got her daughter from Sher Afghan, Ladli Begum, married to one of Jahangir's sons Shahriyar Mirza. When Shah Jahan heard of this marriage, he killed Khusrau who had been a political hostage with him in the Deccan. This was the first time in Mughal history that a brother would kill a brother for the throne.

By then, Shah Jahan had become an unwelcome thorn on the side for Noor Jahan and therefore, for Jahangir as well. In 1622, Shah Jahan staged a rebellion and declared himself the Padshah of Hindustan. His rebellion was shortlived and he submitted to the throne soon after. But an enraged Jahangir declared him bi-daulat—without authority—and he remained in exile in the Deccan. His sons Dara Shikoh and Aurangzeb, then ten and eight years old respectively, were kept as court hostages by Jahangir. Imagine! This is the same Jahangir who had been a doting grandfather and was beside himself when Shah Shuja was suffering from seizures. Shah Jahan's father-in-law, Asaf Khan, now a powerful official, took a stance against the emperor and his own sister Noor Jahan, and continued to back him through this period of uncertainty.

In 1627, Jahangir died. Shah Jahan wasted no time. In a series of bloody encounters, he killed Shahriyar Mirza, Khusrau's sons, and anyone else who could have been an obstacle to his monarchical ambitions. He took away all of Noor Jahan's powers and sent her to Lahore. Finally, on 14 February 1628, after years of military and political efforts, Shah Jahan was crowned the Padshah of Hindustan. Mumtaz Mahal was declared Padshah Begum.

Mumtaz Mahal lived only for a few years as queen. In those years she supported her husband as before. The zenana was under her control. Her older children were now teenagers and she started planning for the wedding of her eldest son Dara Shikoh who was fifteen.

Three years after becoming the padshah, Shah Jahan travelled again to Burhanpur and Mumtaz Mahal, who was pregnant yet again, went with him. It was here, on the night of 16 June 1631, that Mumtaz Mahal gave birth to her fourteenth child, a daughter, Gauhara Begum. Within hours of the birth, her health deteriorated. As she realized that her end was near, she asked her eldest, Jahanara, to bring her husband to her bedside. A distraught and disbelieving Shah Jahan came to her deathbed and soon she breathed her last at the age of thirty-eight.

It is documented that Shah Jahan was beside himself with grief at the death of his beloved companion. He went into mourning and did not appear in court for a week. He wore white clothes—the colour of mourning in Hindustan. It is said that for two years he did not listen to music or wear perfume, jewellery or colourful clothes. His hair slowly turned white and his eyesight was affected by constant shedding of tears. With Mumtaz Mahal's death, he had lost possibly the one person who did not see him as a ruthless monarch but a loving friend.

Jahanara Begum, who was seventeen then, was made the new Padshah Begum. She took over Shah Jahan's zenana with the help of other senior ladies-in-waiting. Mumtaz Mahal was buried temporarily in a deer garden in the Burhanpur fort. A week after her death, Shah Jahan went to read the fatiha at her grave—a customary prayer read on the occasion of death. He continued to do this every Friday as long as her grave remained in Burhanpur.

A Monument Born of Grief

In the days after her death, as he grieved his wife, Shah Jahan started planning her mausoleum. Although there are legends that Mumtaz Mahal asked for a grand memorial to be built on her grave as she lay on her deathbed, this is not documented. It is more likely that Shah Jahan decided to commission a monument in the days after her death while feeling the loss of his constant companion.

Burhanpur was not a suitably large city of the empire like Agra or Lahore. Therefore, it was decided that Mumtaz Mahal's final resting place would be in Agra. Land was acquired on the banks of the Yamuna in Agra from the Raja of Amber.

♦ *Ahukhana in Burhanpur, Madhya Pradesh, where Mumtaz Mahal was buried for six months*

It is against Islamic law to delay burial or transport bodies over long distances. However, it wasn't unusual for the rulers to break some of these rules for the sake of creating monumental landmarks. Six months after her death, Mumtaz Mahal's body was exhumed and escorted by Shah Shuja and her chief lady-in-waiting to Agra.

Planning and construction started on her memorial tomb that would become a symbol of love all over the world. But besides being a tribute to Shah Jahan's greatest love, it was also a part of the Padshah's long-term vision to mark his place in the history of the world. His biographer Abd al-Hamid Lahawari wrote, '…its strength will represent the firmness of the intentions of its builder'.

Mumtaz Mahal did not have Noor Jahan's charisma. She did not write poetry nor build architectural marvels nor own ships. Her legacy was her surviving children, all of whom went on to become important players in Mughal history in the following years. And the Taj Mahal, sheltering her grave, became one of the greatest architectural monuments, symbolizing an emperor's devotion to his wife.

And So the Taj Was Born

The year was 1631, and Mumtaz Mahal was dead. Her husband, the emperor Shah Jahan, who now ruled from Agra, had decided to build a mausoleum like no other for her. It would be a symbol of his love, and at the same time it would bring together some of the finest traditions of Mughal art and architecture. Before Shah Jahan built this wonder, his predecessors had already become known as artistic builders.

Each of the Mughal rulers before Shah Jahan had encouraged a certain type of design which became representative of the era of that particular king. So when the Taj was to be built, it was a culmination of several years of Mughal architecture in India. A monument, placed at the edge of a formal garden, built in a scale that would leave its audience in awe—the Taj Mahal became the most perfect version of Mughal design and art.

The Garden in Paradise

An important aspect of the Taj Mahal is not just the building itself, but the garden in which it is placed. The garden holds several symbolic meanings in the Mughal tradition, and gets its beginnings with the very first Mughal—Babur. The Mughals were descendants of Central Asians and had a long history of nomadic life, living in the outdoors, in tents. This resulted in a love for nature and an interest in bringing the beauty of their natural surroundings into their built environment. One can say that they were naturalists who went on to become accomplished landscape architects.

Babur, having moved to the subcontinent from Central Asia, introduced the garden tradition which was already a part of Persian architecture. The bagh or garden of this style went on to be called the Mughal Gardens. Initially planned as an area for leisure, these gardens became the backbone on which cities, palaces and tombs were planned.

Usually, the garden would be laid out in the shape of a square. This was further divided into four parts. Paved walkways with sunken water channels in them would divide the main square into four equal-sized squares. The centre of the garden would be occupied by a building—a garden pavilion or a tomb or a pool. Around the square garden would be a wall. This kind of garden was referred to by Babur as the chahar bagh. Or Charbagh—a four-part garden.

The Mughals built different kinds of variants of the Charbagh. These were then simply called bagh. One version of the Mughal bagh was the terrace garden. Laid out on hilly terrain, usually with mountain springs watering the gardens,

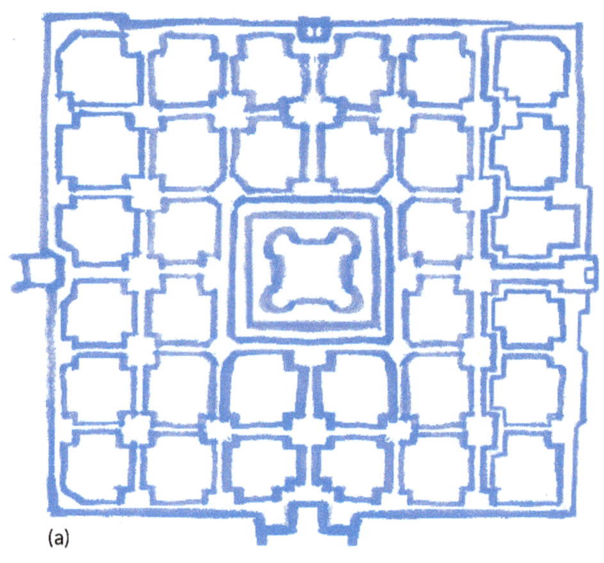

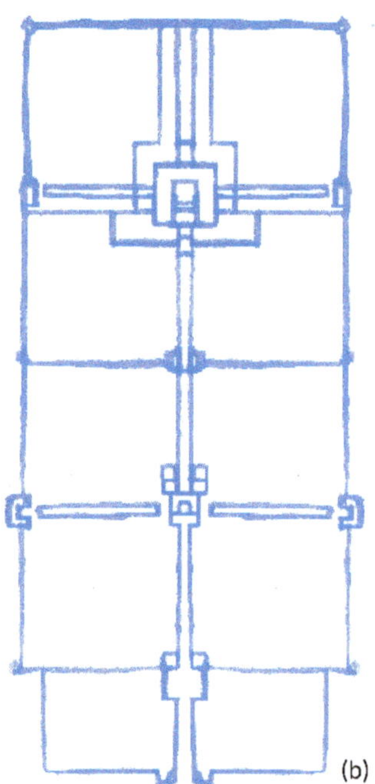

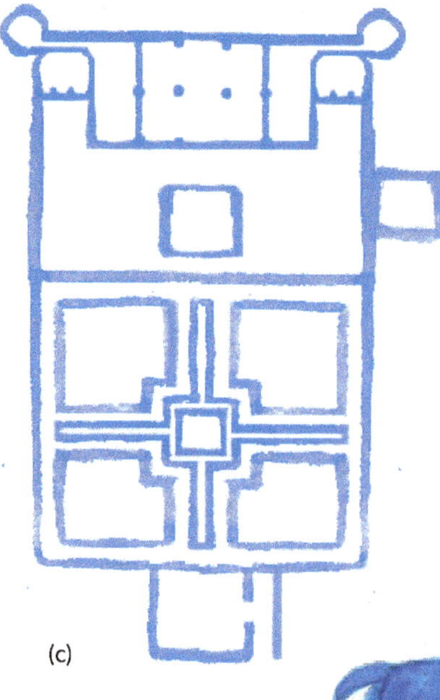

- *Three types of charbagh*

a) Cross-axial; Humayun's Tomb, Delhi
b) Terraced; Shalimar Bagh, Kashmir
c) Waterfront; Lal Mahal, Bari

these were leisure complexes for the royal family. Some were built in Kabul and Kashmir. The gardens had beautiful pavilions for spending time outdoors. The central dividing axis would be a walkway with a sunken water channel where the water from the springs flowed. Shalimar Bagh, built by Shah Jahan, in Srinagar, Kashmir is one such garden.

◆ *Shalimar Bagh*

The third type of bagh was the waterfront garden. Here, a river would be the main source of water for the gardens. The main building would be on the riverfront, usually on a raised platform. On the landward side of this building would be the Charbagh garden with walkways and water channels. In Agra and in Shahjahanabad (present-day Old Delhi) the waterfront garden design was used along the banks of the Yamuna. The Taj Mahal is the best example of the waterfront garden.

Garden to Garden-City

The first Charbagh built by Babur in India was in Agra, next to the Yamuna river. The symmetrical design of the gardens introduced a new way of city planning in India. It became a blueprint for planning and building cities. Babur wrote, 'The people of Hind who had never seen grounds planned so symmetrically and thus laid out, called the side of the Jun (Yamuna) where residences were Kabul.'

Humayun moved his seat of power to Delhi but could not build much there as he had to flee to Persia. It was Akbar, who moved back to Agra and started developing the city. The riverfront became the main area of development. He granted several pieces of land to his favoured officials who made grand mansions and gardens along the river.

Under Jahangir, the riverfront gardens developed even further in Agra with several baghs along the river. Noor Jahan built the beautiful tomb for her parents (Itmad-ud-daulah's tomb) as a classic Charbagh with the tomb pavilion at the centre of the layout.

When Shah Jahan moved to Agra as the new padshah, he renamed it as Akbarabad. Under his administration, Akbarabad grew to be a flourishing and rich town, often written about by travellers and historians as one of the grandest cities of the world of the time. The main development continued along

the river, making it a long and narrow city. The wealthy families preferred plots that faced the river to take advantage of the view and so they could develop beautiful gardens using the river as a source of water.

The Last Resting Spot of Kings

The gardens became the backdrop for most of the buildings that the Mughals built. Starting from leisure pavilions, palaces and towns were placed amidst the beautifully manicured, symmetrical baghs, planted with trees that bore flowers and fruits. But across generations, the Mughal kings also built several landmark tombs.

Each of the great Mughal padshahs built tombs for their fathers. As Jahangir wrote, 'A thousand blessings on a son who has made such a tomb for his father.'

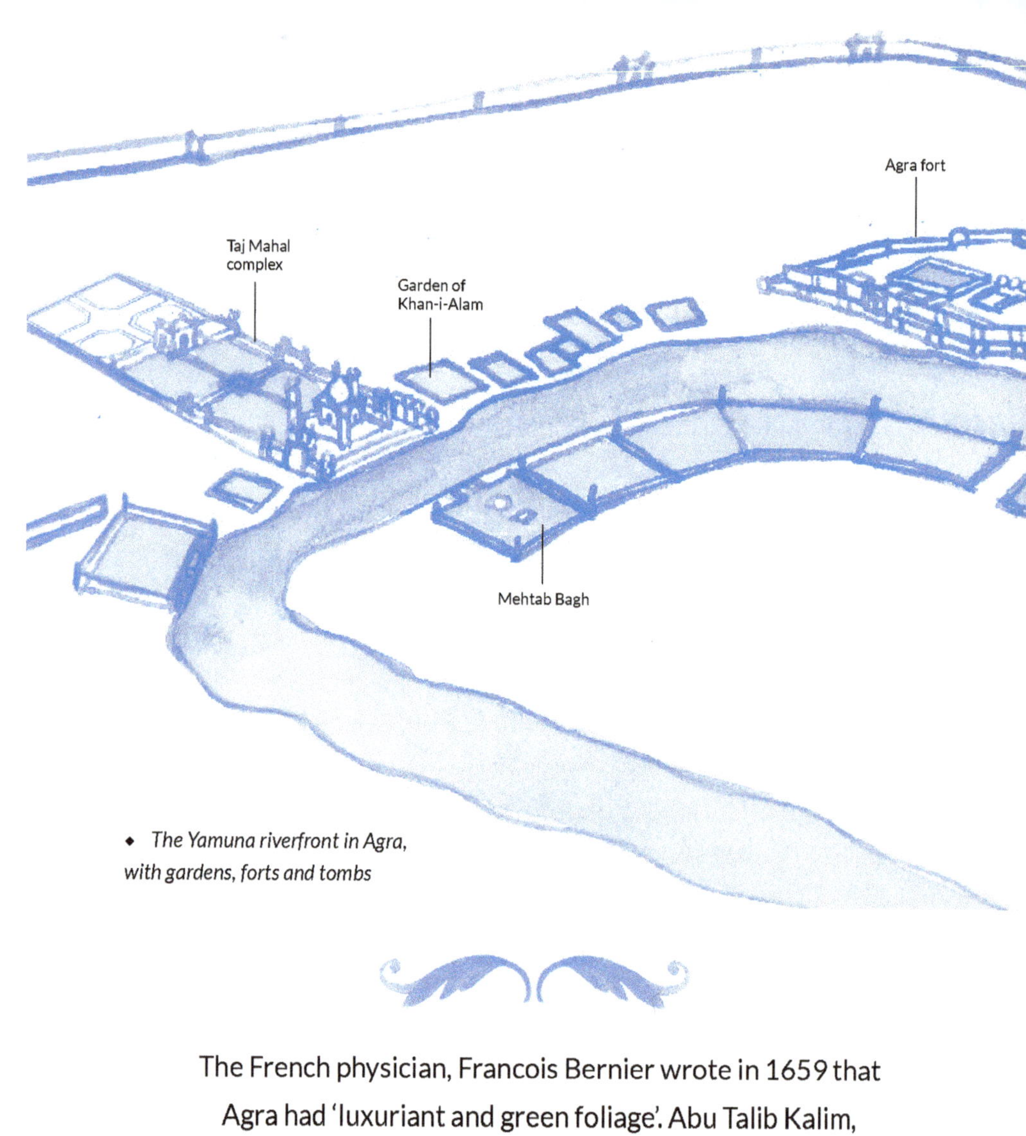

◆ *The Yamuna riverfront in Agra, with gardens, forts and tombs*

The French physician, Francois Bernier wrote in 1659 that Agra had 'luxuriant and green foliage'. Abu Talib Kalim, Shah Jahan's court poet wrote a long poem on the city, describing its beauty. Here are a few lines that describe the riverfront of Akbarabad:

'The heart attracting buildings lie on both sides of the river:

Like the face and the mirror, they are opposite each other.

The buildings are so lovely

That the river does not want to pass by.'

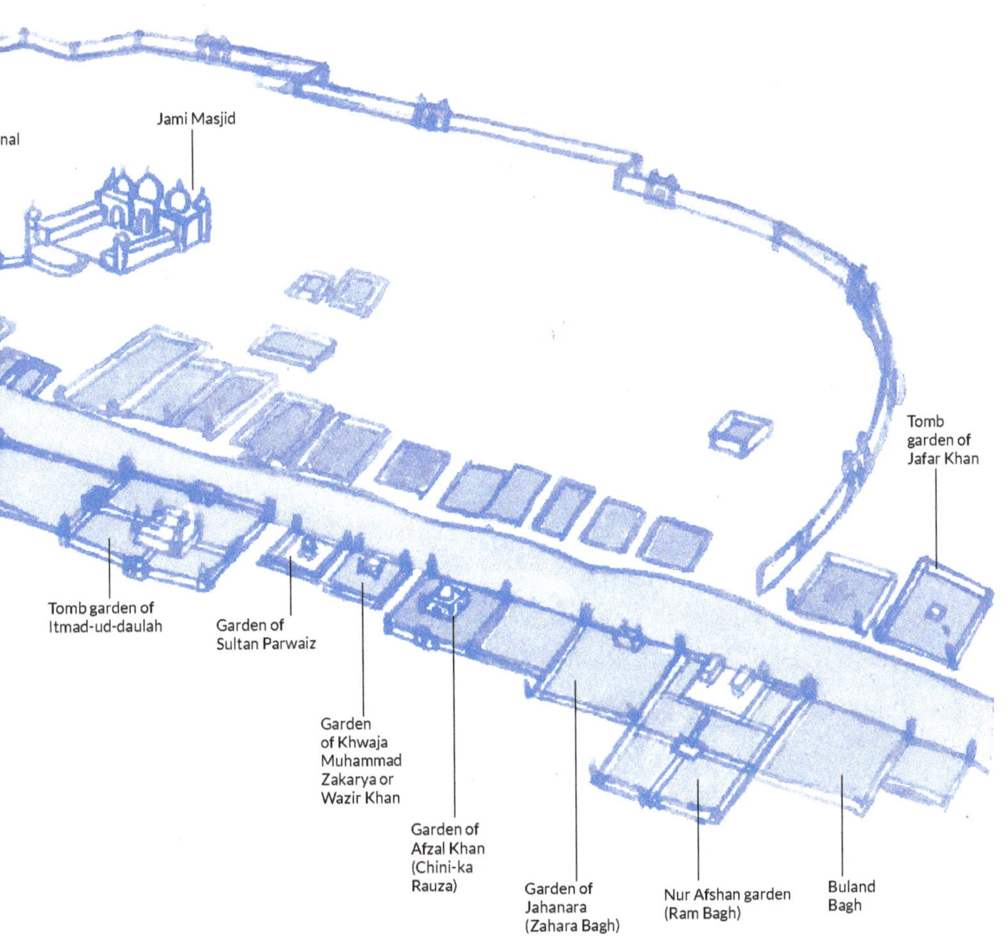

The building of monumental mausoleums was a contradiction of Islamic laws. The Quran said that building structures over tombs was unacceptable as these could become pilgrimage spots, which in turn would be a form of idol worship. But this was disregarded quite regularly by the Muslim rulers in Hindustan. Instead, tombs became expressions of respect, love and political supremacy.

Timur, the forefather of the Mughals, was buried in a beautiful tomb with double domes in Samarqand, Central Asia. It is a grand structure clad with blue and green tiles.

Babur's tomb was open to the sky and was according to Muslim tradition. It is believed that Babur's tomb was originally an austere monument of a stone block. However, later Akbar and Jahangir added elements like a terrace garden and a stone inscription to make it appropriate for a Mughal king.

Humayun was buried in Delhi and as described earlier, his wife, Bega Begum, constructed a tomb with the help of Persian masons and architects.

Humayun's tomb was an early example of a tomb set in the Charbagh layout. The building was at the centre of the Charbagh. The cenotaph, which marks the spot of the actual grave, is in a lower chamber and placed on a high plinth with vaults on four sides. Humayun's tomb was the first major Mughal building to use a combination of red sandstone and white marble. This combination went on to become a feature of Mughal architecture. The tomb was topped by a large double-vaulted dome.

Humayun's tomb broke all the rules that Islam has made for burial spots. The scale of this building made it monumental, thus defying the rule that graves should be simple structures. Its grandeur and rich construction made it a place where people would come to pay homage to the buried emperor. This again was a contradiction of Islamic rules that burials should not become places of pilgrimage.

Nevertheless, a combination of its Indo-Persian design and its grand scale made Humayun's tomb a trendsetter in Mughal architecture.

What is the double-vaulted dome?

This means that the dome is double-layered. There is one layer inside, which serves as the ceiling to the interior of the building. The other layer is the outer one which crowns the building. The outer layer can be raised to a greater height which makes the external appearance of the building very grand. Humayun's tomb had the first double-layered dome in India.

After this, the tradition of grand mausoleums continued as Jahangir built a beautiful tomb for Akbar at Sikandra, near Agra. It was designed by Jahangir himself. The structure has the same vaulted plinth as Humayun's tomb. But the rest of the design is very different, and shows distinct Hindu influences, especially in the use of chhatris.

In Akbar's tomb the cenotaph is open to sky. Red sandstone and marble was used in this building too and it, too, was surrounded by a garden. Jahangir wrote in his memoirs that the original design by the architects did not meet his approval. The construction had already started, but he had the structure torn down and rebuilt as per his own design.

Jahangir's tomb was built by his wife, Noor Jahan, in

A **chhatri** is a domed pavilion used commonly in Rajasthani architecture. It means umbrella. Chhatris could be memorials built on the site where the cremation of an important person was held. It is also used to refer to the small pavilions that mark the corners and roof of the entrance of a major building. These are decorative pavilions and do not have any function. The Mughals adopted this element of Hindu architecture to decorate their palaces, forts and tombs.

◆ *An example of a chhatri*

Lahore. He had willed that his tomb be simple, like Babur's, and be left open to the sky. Therefore, the final structure is similar to Akbar's tomb—a cenotaph on a vaulted platform—but with less embellishments and with four minarets at the corners. Akbar's and Jahangir's tombs paved the way for new ideas in tomb architecture and they were appropriately grand to suit a Mughal padshah, yet with a degree of simplicity that allowed the grave to be open to sky.

Shah Jahan's son Aurangzeb was a traditionalist. He ruled against visiting tombs and building grand monuments over graves. His own grave is a simple stone slab, open to sky at the dargah of the Sufi saint Sheikh Burhan-ud-din in Khuldabad, near Aurangabad. His sister Jahanara was also buried in a simple grave in Delhi at the dargah of Nizamuddin Auliya. After a few generations of grandeur in their burials, with Aurangzeb, this tradition of grand mausoleums ended.

However, before that, Shah Jahan created the grandest example of a funerary palace garden with the Taj Mahal. By the time Mumtaz Mahal died, Agra was a beautiful garden city. It was an appropriate resting place for the begum. Combining his heritage of building in the garden and his ambition to leave behind a symbol of his reign as a great ruler, Shah Jahan started planning the memorial for his favourite wife.

Shah Jahan, the Architect

Shah Jahan was a great builder and throughout his reign he commissionned, designed and constructed great landmarks of architecture. In all his work, whether as emperor, administrator or a patron of art and culture, Shah Jahan liked to be in control. He personally supervised all proceedings and projects. He was a perfectionist and for him architecture was a representation of the emperor himself. He believed that monuments and buildings would remain as memorials of the era. This reflected an Arabic saying, 'Our monuments will tell of us.'

To enable him to build such everlasting monuments, he employed a large team of architects and advisers. His historians have written accounts of his style of working as the chief patron of architecture. His master architects would present proposals to him and as Qazwini wrote, 'And since his most pure mind is inclined entirely towards building…he attends to it fully by creating most of the designs himself and also by making appropriate changes to whatever the architects have thought out.'

As a prince and later as the emperor, Shah Jahan built several buildings and complexes. He rebuilt the palaces in Agra and Lahore; Shahjahanabad in Delhi was a new seat of power built by him; Shalimar Bagh in Kashmir was a beautiful formal garden made under his patronage. He built several mosques, the largest being the Jama Masjid in Delhi and also the beautiful Moti Masjid in the Agra Fort. Jahangir's tomb in Lahore was constructed by him, and Noor Jahan supervised it. The Taj Mahal was the crowning glory of his architectural projects.

While Shah Jahan had a team of architects, there is no record of a single architect or a smaller team of designers being given the credit of designing this architectural marvel.

It was Shah Jahan who was the central authority and the main creator of the Taj Mahal. While the planning of the Taj Mahal was done by the group of architects, Shah Jahan would supervise the process in great detail.

As the designing of Mumtaz Mahal's final resting place progressed, Shah Jahan and his team incorporated Mughal elements in their most polished form. Visualized as Mumtaz Mahal's home in Paradise, the final design was perfect in its execution, as if without human error. The Charbagh, which had been introduced by his great-great-grandfather Babur, became the paradisical garden in which the queen's mausoleum would stand. The design of the Taj Mahal incorporated elements of Mughal architecture, local materials, different artistic traditions including those derived from Hindu art—making the Taj Mahal a wonder of the world.

A Walk Around the Taj

Here we are, standing at the large arched gate that is the entrance to the Taj Mahal. If we look straight ahead, we see the white marble structure, glimmering and shimmering in the sunlight. This first sight of the monument that has been photographed and filmed by so many, takes the breath away. Pristine, beautifully symmetric, the Taj stands there, as it has for centuries, drawing in the eye and imprinting itself on every soul that sees it.

The stupendous beauty of the Taj was achieved thanks to detailed planning by Shah Jahan. For him, it was not just a mausoleum for a favourite queen, but also an expression of the very pinnacle of Mughal architecture. The Mughals had been in India now for two hundred years, and the Taj, Shah Jahan had decided, would epitomize their sense of beauty and aesthetics through brick and mortar. With the Taj Mahal, he set out to do something that would outdo everything attempted before in scale and grandeur.

What makes the Taj remarkable is that each element in its construction had deep thought and meaning behind it. Shah Jahan visualized the structure as a representation of Mumtaz Mahal's house in the gardens of Jannat, or Paradise.

Jannat is an Arabic word. The Quran describes Jannat as an eternal garden where there are springs of fresh water, milk, honey and wine. There are trees providing eternal shade in this garden. It's a beautiful place that is full of rewards for the faithful. Since the origin of Islam is in the arid regions of western Asia, a walled garden with shade and water would certainly be a desired luxury.

The main structure of the Taj stands on a terrace built right by the river. Agra, in Mughal times, was a riverfront city, meaning several mansions and leisure pavilions were built on the riverbank, where they received fresh and cool air from the Yamuna.

To build the Taj, Shah Jahan chose a site that belonged to Raja Man Singh of Amber. At the time, the area was in the ownership of the Raja's grandson, Jai Singh. In exchange for the land, Shah Jahan gifted four mansions in Agra to Jai Singh. It is recorded that Jai Singh wanted to give the land as a gift, but Shah Jahan insisted on a transaction so that in the future there would be no confusion regarding land ownership.

The location of this land was at the bend of the Yamuna river which allowed the grave to be aligned perfectly towards Mecca, the holiest Muslim shrine. From the main fort, the location gave a perfect framing. And the Yamuna with its freshly flowing Himalayan water would be the centre of Shah Jahan's vision—the river symbolizing the fresh flowing waters of Jannat, on whose bank would be laid the departed queen.

Mumtaz Mahal had died in distant Burhanpur, far from Agra. She had been interred there according to Islamic customs, soon after her death. Once the site for the mausoleum was identified, her body was brought by her son Shah Shuja and long-time companion Satti-un-Nisa Khanum from Burhanpur. At the site in Agra, she was given a temporary burial spot and a pavilion was built over it to 'protect her chastity'. The construction started with the laying of the foundation of the riverside terrace.

The planning and design of the Taj Mahal was done by people who were extremely skilled in visualizing and planning. So who were the architects? We read earlier that there are no official records naming the architects of the Taj Mahal. But there is circumstantial evidence that throws up a name.

Official history of the time names Shah Jahan as the undisputed brain behind the conceptualizing of the Taj Mahal complex. It is assumed that he employed a team of master builders and craftsmen to advise him and work out the technical and artistic details that he possibly sketched out for them.

While there is no definite record of an appointed architect for the Taj Mahal, there is some evidence that the main architect was Ustad Ahmed Lahori. Lahori is mentioned as the designer of Shahjahanabad in the official history of Shah Jahan's reign. His son Luft Allah wrote in his book that his father designed the Taj Mahal and Shahjahanabad. Since one half of that claim seems to be confirmed in official accounts, it is assumed that the son's claim that he designed both these projects is possibly true. Lahori's grave in Aurangabad also describes him as the architect of the Taj, as well as the fort and the Jama Masjid in Delhi.

Lahori was an architect, engineer, mathematician and astronomer. That makes him nearly as multifaceted as Leonardo da Vinci, the renaissance polymath from Italy. When we look at the design of the Taj Mahal, it is apparent that all his qualifications were remarkably utilized. The planning and design of the Taj Mahal balanced geometry, mathematics, engineering and aesthetic beauty in perfect harmony.

European visitors of the 17th century like Sebastian Manrique suggested that the Taj Mahal was a building of such beauty that it could not have been designed by anyone other than an European. He named a Venetian goldsmith, Geronimo Veroneo, as the architect. While Geronimo did attend Shah Jahan's court, there is no evidence to prove his involvement in the creation of the Taj.

In the Islamic world, the role of
the architect-engineer was closely
associated with the mathematician.
In the West, on the other hand,
the role of the architect came
into existence through a process
whereby designer-builders slowly
distinguished themselves from the
ranks of builders and craftsmen.
Islamic architects were often
distinguished mathematicians.

What is recorded is that Shah Jahan led a team of architects to plan the Taj Mahal and most of his other projects. He held regular meetings with them. His official biographer, Lahauri, wrote that he 'made appropriate alterations to whatever the skillful architects designed after many thoughts, and asked competent questions.' Royal historians claimed that the emperor was the supreme architect.

The Plan

Let us now imagine we are birds and take wings to hover over the Taj Mahal. Fluttering high up in the air, we see that the entire site on which it is built is rectangular in shape. The main mausoleum is located at the northern end, which is also the riverside. As the Yamuna snakes its way past, we can spot steps leading down to the river from here and the Taj Mahal sitting on a raised terrace.

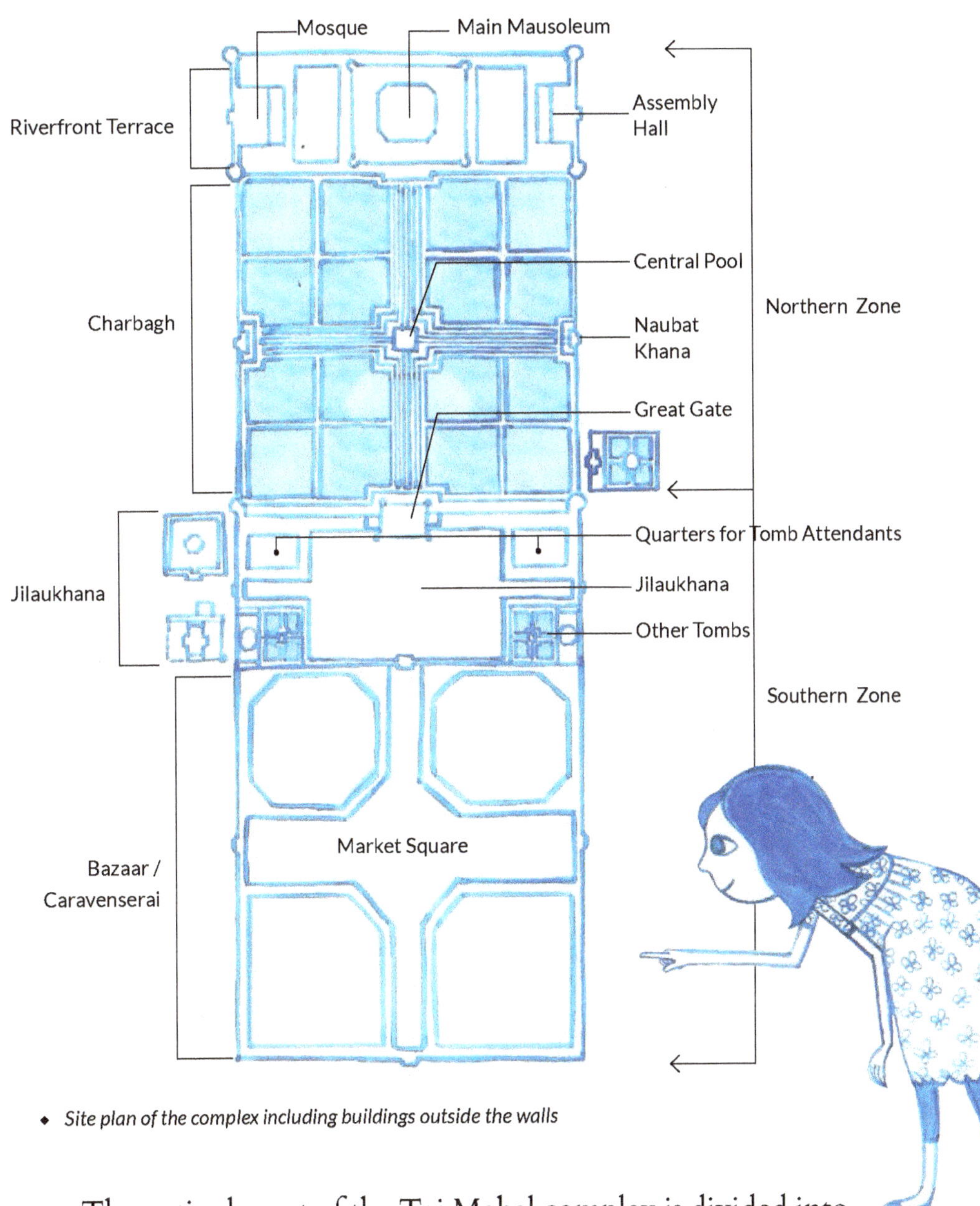

◆ *Site plan of the complex including buildings outside the walls*

The entire layout of the Taj Mahal complex is divided into two zones. The northern zone consists of the mausoleum, a mosque, an assembly hall and a Charbagh garden. This is the funerary part of the complex, which is the sacred or spiritual area with the grave and its surrounding structures that are meant for prayers and paying respect. The southern zone of the complex

◆ *Arcades in the jilaukhana*

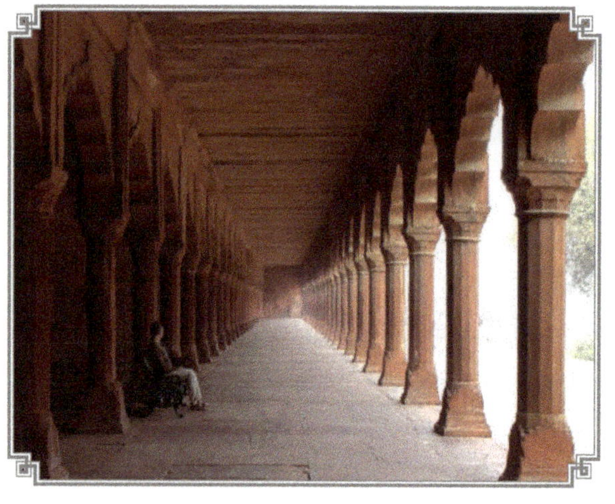

is called the 'worldly' zone. This includes a forecourt called the Jilaukhana, quarters for tomb attendants called Khawasspuras, smaller tombs of other queens of Shah Jahan called Saheli Burj and the bazaar streets to the extreme south.

In the original plan, the southern half of the complex was a large bazaar complex with shops and caravanserais. This area was divided into four courts, reflecting the Charbagh plan

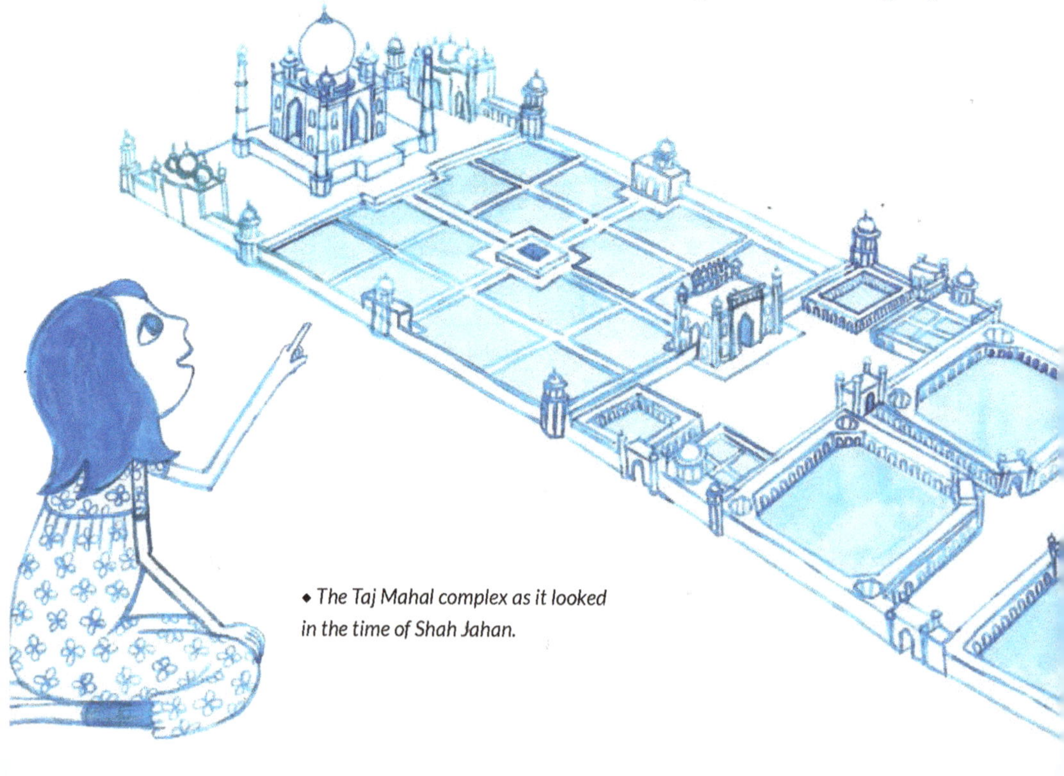

◆ *The Taj Mahal complex as it looked in the time of Shah Jahan.*

of the Taj. But now this complex is lost. The modern city of Agra has grown right up to here. However, we can still imagine what it must have been like to be a visitor to the Taj in Mughal times. In the bazaar, amidst the bustle, one could stand and view the monument in all its magnificence.

• *The modern city of Agra comes right up to the gates of the Taj Mahal now*

While this is the obvious layout of the Taj Mahal complex as we see it today, there are possibilities that we are seeing only half of Shah Jahan's grand plan.

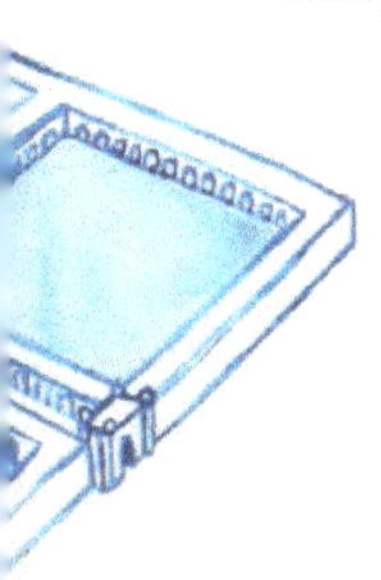

A Twin Taj?

Today it appears as though the Taj Mahal complex was designed to be viewed from the main gate on the southern side. But it is interesting to note that the emperor Shah Jahan never entered the mausoleum complex from here. The royal family approached the mausoleum from the riverside. They came in barges which they boarded at the Agra Fort—their residence—and alighted at the riverside steps of the Taj Mahal. They climbed the staircases to the top of the platform, paid their respects at the crypt, possibly rested for a while in the rooms overlooking the river below the platform, and departed by boat. It was the river that connected the living with the departed—from the Fort to the Illumined Tomb.

Therefore, it is possible that the river of Jannat that was meant to flow past Mumtaz Mahal's grave is the Yamuna with the freshly melted snow from the mountains and not the water channels in the Charbagh that adorned the gardens of the Taj.

On the other side of the river, facing the Taj Mahal, lies Mehtab Bagh. A Charbagh garden in ruins today, it has been said that Shah Jahan had planned a black Taj Mahal as his own tomb here. There is nothing to support this theory. But Mehtab Bagh may have been part of Shah Jahan's original plan in a more symbolic interpretation of Jannat. Mehtab Bagh also has a Charbagh layout with a riverside terrace and its proportions are similar to the Taj Mahal.

What has emerged, through new studies and archaeological

◆ *The plan of the Taj Mahal with the river and Mehtab Bagh*

diggings, is that the garden across the river was probably a part of a larger plan where two Charbaghs lay on either side of the river. The white mausoleum of the Taj Mahal would then adorn the paradisical river on one side. The other side of the river had a large octagonal pool which would reflect the Taj Mahal perfectly on a moonlit night.

The cardinal directions in this layout were perfect. The Yamuna flowing from east to west, the main canals of the two baghs flowing north to south, with the mausoleum at the centre. If this was the original plan, it automatically makes the entire concept of the mausoleum in Jannat far grander. In fact,

◆ *A view of the Taj Mahal from Mehtab Bagh*

it was double the size of what we had assumed the original plan was, based on what we see today.

A grand plan of this scale would be expected from a builder like Shah Jahan. His vision was extraordinary and his intent was to create masterpieces of architecture that were symbolic of his stature as one of the greatest Mughlas.

Let's Walk in

Today, the Taj Mahal complex is entered through gates that lie to the east and west. These lead to the Jilaukhana, or a forecourt. The word jilaukhana means 'in front of the house'.

The forecourt is a grand space. In earlier days, it would be abuzz when visitors came to the Taj, for it is here that they would alight from their horses and elephants before entering the main complex. It was also used for the ceremonial gathering on the first death anniversary of Mumtaz Mahal.

Interestingly, the element of a **forecourt** was introduced by Shah Jahan in Mughal architecture. Before this, their buildings did not have such a space. Shah Jahan realized that without a forecourt, there were no formal areas in palaces, forts and other places for people to gather, to dismount and to be received formally. Without forecourts, palaces and forts saw traffic congestion and chaos. In fact, the Agra Fort, too, lacked a forecourt and this was much lamented in texts by historians like Kanbo.

The Taj forecourt has two enclosures. One enclosure has the living quarters of the tomb attendants or khawasspuras. Here, the people who looked after the tombs and those who read the holy scriptures resided. Jean-Baptiste Tavernier, a French merchant and traveller, described in his account of his travels to Agra how he witnessed the Quran being recited here, day and night, for Mumtaz Mahal.

◆ *A view of the gardens from the Taj Mahal*

◆ *The main entrance of the Taj Mahal*

The other enclosure within the forecourt has two tombs. These are believed to have been built for Shah Jahan's other wives. Records are not very clear about the identity of these two women, but popular belief is that they were called Akbarabadi Mahal and Fatehpuri Mahal. These tombs are also placed within small charbaghs. The tombs are called Saheli Burj (tower of the female friend).

On the northern side of the jilaukhana is the gate that leads to the main complex.

The great gate or the darwaza-i-rauza is a large ceremonial gate. It has a tall central arch called pishtaq. On either side of the pishtaq are two tiers of smaller arches. A similar gate can be seen at Akbar's tomb in Sikandra. The corners of the

◆ *Details of the main entrance*

gate have four towers. As you walk in, you find that the cross section of the gate has several smaller arches and niches on the walls. The central part of the gate is mounted with cupolas, or small domes. The entire structure is clad in red sandstone and white marble, and adorned with inlay work of flowers and geometrical patterns in the marble.

Take a step in from here, and you get the first view of the Taj Mahal. It is a spectacular sight as the layout of the complex ensures that this first viewing of the mausoleum is from a point that underlines the Taj's overwhelming beauty.

A Garden Beautiful

We have read about how the Mughals loved to lay out

gardens. From Persia and Central Asia they had carried with them memories of beautiful gardens that sprang out from the surrounding dry lands. In India, they set about creating their own versions of the perfect garden. This needed meticulous planning and attention to detail. This vision of the garden reached its perfection with what Shah Jahan created at the Taj.

Here, the garden was designed as a reflection of the garden in paradise with trees that flower and bear fruit and water channels symbolizing the rivers of water, milk and honey that flow in Jannat. Shah Jahan's historian, Lahauri, called it the Bagh-i-firdaus-a'in or 'Paradise-like garden'.

The garden is a large square with two perpendicular walkways that divide it into four parts or quadrants. Narrow walkways further divide each of these sub-quadrants. Thus, the whole garden is divided into sixteen sub-quadrants. Just like a neat jigsaw puzzle, isn't it?

The two main walkways intersect at the centre of the garden. Here, there is a raised marble platform within which is a pool or hauz. The water in the pool is symbolic of the heavenly Kausar, or the river that flows in Paradise, as described by the Prophet. There are five fountains in this pool. Today, there are four benches on each side of the square that forms the hauz. These were added much later by Lord Curzon, the British Viceroy of India. Curzon was fascinated by the Taj and did much to revive and conserve the structure. But more on that later.

These two walkways have water channels running along

the centre with a line of fountains. Sandstone strips and ornamental borders in geometric shapes of regular and oblong stars flank this canal.

One of these walkways that runs north-south, connects the great gate and the tomb. It also divides the garden into two nearly equal halves. This is the main central axis of the complex. When you stand towards the gate-end of the walkway, you can see the perfect symmetry and balance of the design.

The other walkway, that runs east-west, connects two pavilions. These are called Garden-Wall Pavilions or Naubat Khana (loosely translated as Drum-House). This is also a symmetrical layout.

◆ *Garden-Wall Pavilions or Naubat Khana*

◆ *The Taj Mahal with a profusion of trees, as originally planted and planned*

The garden would get water from the Yamuna. An aqueduct brought up water from the river to the western wall of the garden and then earthenware pipes were used to distribute the water.

The trees in the garden have changed drastically from the time of the Mughals. Not much is known about the type of trees and plants that were originally used. From some accounts it appears that cypress, poplar and almond trees were planted. Flowers like iris, tulip, rose, marigold and poppies were popular in Mughal times, and we can imagine that these were planted here too. Travellers in the 18th and 19th centuries have described orange trees near the Taj, and

◆ *The trees around Taj Mahal today*

other accounts suggest that fruit-bearing trees like pineapple, pomelo, mango, guava and lime adorned the gardens. There are records that the fruit and aromatic herbs from the garden were sold. The revenue from such sales went to the waqf or trust that maintained the complex, set up by Shah Jahan.

What we also know is that the planting was not formal as it is today. The foliage was profuse, almost hiding the lower parts of the main building. If you can imagine, with the lush greenery, a viewer seeing the Taj Mahal from the gate would probably have seen just the shimmering white dome, almost floating above the trees. What a mesmerizing sight that must have been!

Looking at the Mausoleum

The garden leads up to the focal point of the entire complex. The north-south walkway ends at the raised riverfront terrace. At its centre sits the mausoleum with four minarets at the four corners of a platform. On either side of this, again following symmetry, are two structures—a mosque on the left and an assembly hall on the right.

The raised platform on which the mausoleum is erected is one of the grandest riverfront terraces built by the Mughals.

Clad in red sandstone, it is elaborately decorated with relief work in sandstone and inlay work in marble.

On the riverside, the façade of the terrace is decorated with a row of blind arches. Why are these arches blind? Because they do not have openings, instead they are closed with masonry and then decorated with motifs of flowers, vases or palm trees.

At the foot of the terrace, next to the river, were landing steps. These led to stairs that took you up to the level of the mausoleum. Shah Jahan would arrive by boat from across the

◆ *Blind arches*

Inlay and relief are two techniques of sculpture. In the case of the Taj Mahal, the material used for both the techniques is stone—marble or red sandstone.

Relief comes from the word Latin verb relevo, or to raise. A sculpture in relief looks as though the sculpted material has been raised above the background plane. When a relief is cut from a flat surface of stone the background is chiseled away, leaving the sculpture or design raised. As you can imagine, this means a lot of chiseling and therefore a time-consuming and painstaking process.

Inlay work involves cutting out the design into the surface of the stone and then filling the carved portions with other material—other stones, gems or paint.

The inlaid material and the base stone is on the same plane when the work is completed, i.e. there is no raised surface.

river and use this route to visit his wife's grave. Sadly, today one cannot retrace the emperor's path because the landing is covered by silt and sand.

Below the marble platform is a gallery of rooms. This is called the tahkhana. There are seven large rooms connected alternately to six small square rooms. At one time, these rooms were used by royal visitors to rest when they came to the tomb. The rooms used to open to the river through arches. These arches were closed later and became 'blind'. Today, the access to the rooms from the platform above is also closed.

The marble platform was called the takhtgah or kursi, meaning throne. Calling the tomb platform a throne gives it a royal feel. The actual burial chamber having a grand platform built above it is a Mughal feature. We saw how Humayun's tomb has a similar arrangement where a cenotaph at a higher level marks the location of the actual grave below.

The platform is a square with the four minarets at the corners. The huge platform is clad in marble—this is quite a

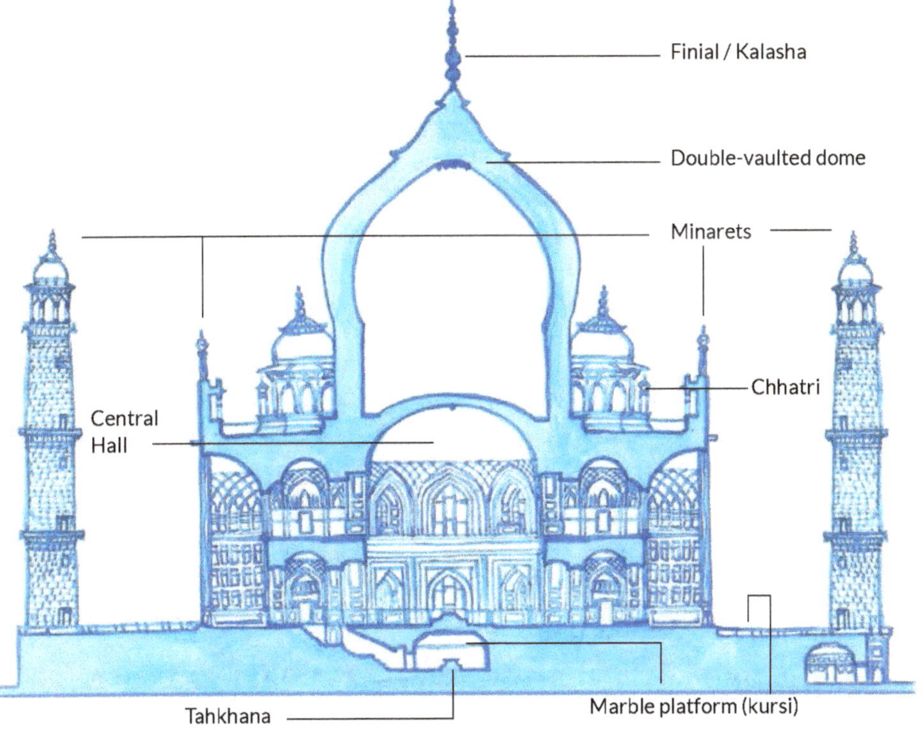

unique feature for the entire platform to be covered in marble. In earlier instances sandstone or other such stone were used.

Two flights of stairs on the south side of the platform bring you from the garden to the level of the mausoleum.

And finally now we are looking at the climax of the entire complex—a building clad in pure white marble that sits on the kursi. Shah Jahan called it the Imarat-i-rauza munauwara or 'the building of the illumined tomb'. The Taj Mahal's perfect symmetry of every element and the white marble, are all signs of purity.

The mausoleum is designed on a plan known as the hasht bihisht plan used by the Mughals frequently. In this, the octagon is divided into four by two imaginary, intersecting lines in a cross (+). These lines are called the two axes. Where these two imaginary axes intersect, at the centre of the octagon, the central octagonal hall is located. This has a domed ceiling. This central hall is connected through passages to four rectangular halls at the periphery of each side of the square. Another cross pattern (x) again divides the octagon. This x is made by intersecting corridors that connect to four rooms, one at each corner. These rooms are octagonal in plan.

All the passages that criss-cross the building are interconnected, so a visitor can walk along these passages and take a full circle of the interiors of the main floor of the Taj Mahal, peeping into every room as they walk.

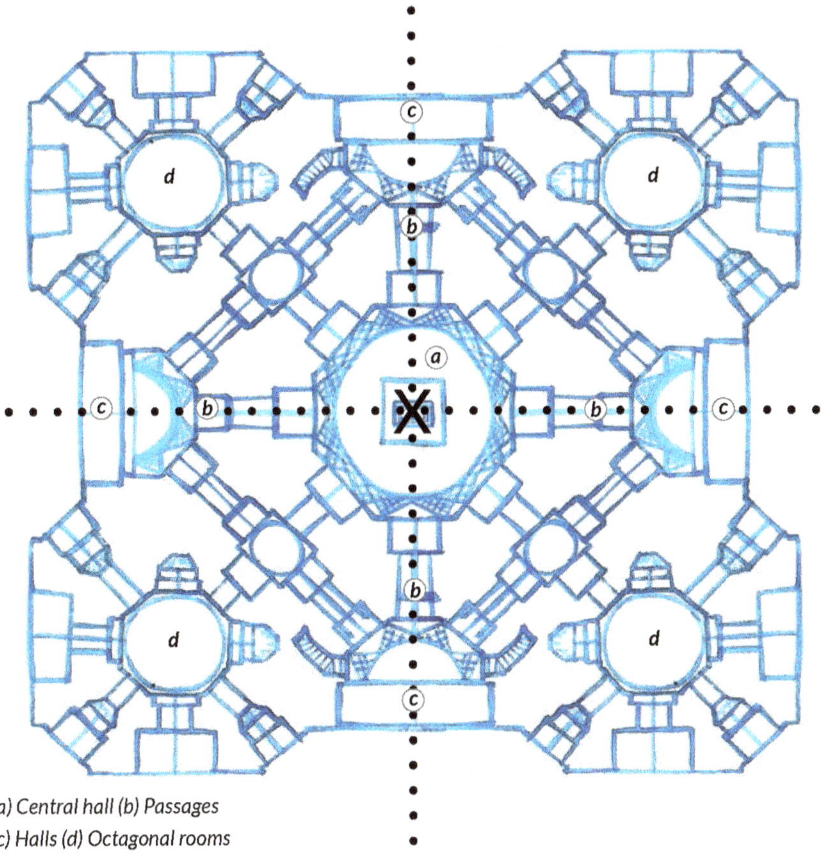

(a) Central hall (b) Passages
(c) Halls (d) Octagonal rooms

◆ *Hasht bihisht plan of Humayun's Tomb*

Hasht Bihisht is a Persian term meaning Eight Paradises. It was a planning tool, used by the Mughals in the 16th and 17th century for designing pavilions and tombs. It consists typically of a square or a rectangle. Sometimes the corners are chamfered, or cut, to form an octagon. This type of octagon with four long sides and four short sides was called a Musamman Baghdadi or a Baghdadi Octagon by the Mughals.

Humayun's Tomb in Delhi is built on this principle. The Taj Mahal has the Hasht Bihisht plan interpreted to perfection.

The building as we see from outside is called its elevation, in architectural terms. As we discussed, the bird's eyes view of the Taj Mahal has eight sides.

The Exterior of the Mausoleum

The mausoleum sits on a plinth, or a pedestal. This pedestal is covered with marble and is decorated with carvings of leaves and buds hanging from stems. The entire base of the plinth has a repetitive pattern of such carvings.

Each of the four walls on the external façade has a central arch (pishtaq). Framing the central arch, as decoration on the

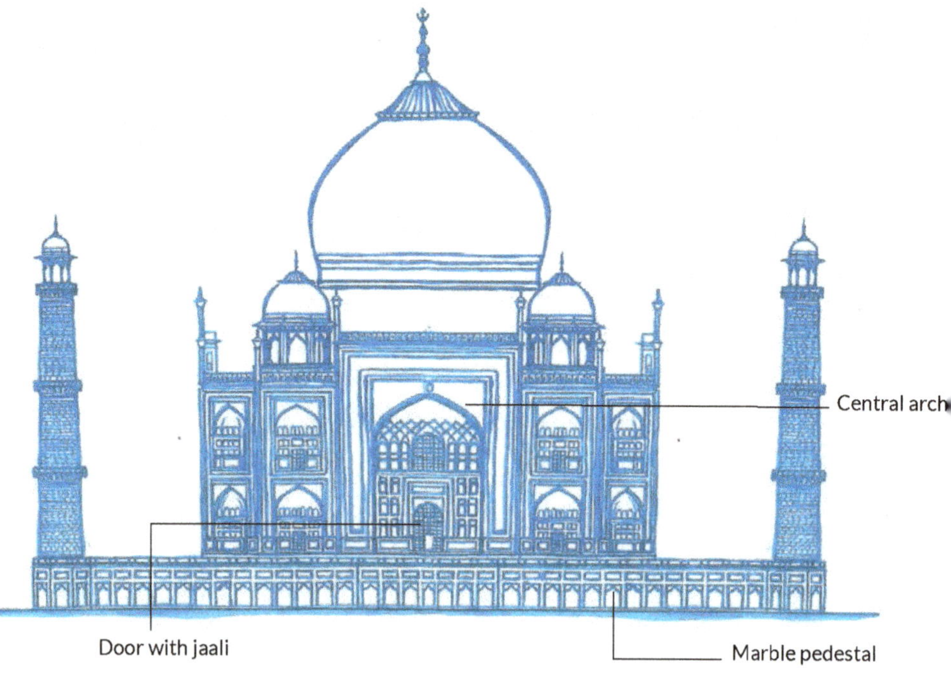

◆ *South elevation of the mausolem, with its marble platform and flanking minarets*

wall, is a rectangular band which is made of Quranic verses inscribed on the marble.

These verses are about divine forgiveness and how the faithful would be rewarded in Paradise. Today as we look at these inscriptions above the main entrance of the mausoleum, it seems like these were put here because Shah Jahan built the mausoleum as a representation of Paradise itself and the verses at the entrance depicted the purity of the building.

The inner wall of the arch has another interesting feature. There are horizontal bands of decorations in the form of delicate floral patterns, carved in relief. The interesting bit is that none of these flowers can be identified! These seem to be inventions of the craftsmen and sometimes the blossoms and leaves on a single plant may actually belong to different species. But like everything else at the Taj, the arrangement of the carvings is symmetrical and follows a pattern.

Interior Details of the Mausoleum

Now we are standing in the central domed hall of the mausoleum. It is majestic and awe-inspiring—the culmination of the mausoleum. Octagonal in shape, each side of this hall is 24 feet long. It is surrounded by eight niches, all equal in size, with arches. And above all of this is the grand apex of the dome. It is decorated with detailed inlay work and from it hangs a bronze lamp. Here we meet Lord Curzon again, for

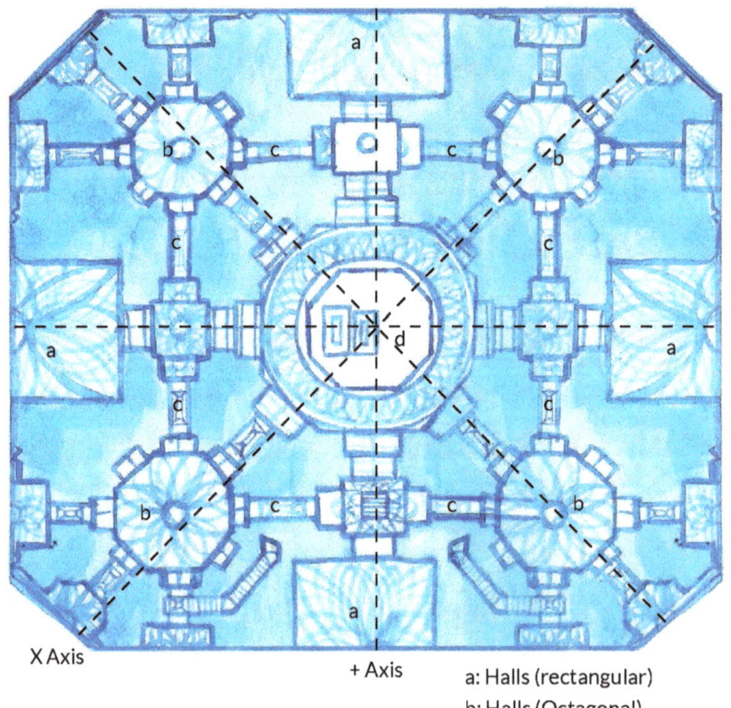

• A plan of the ground floor of the Taj Mahal

this lamp was added here by him. Inlaid with gold and silver, it was made in Egypt and shipped over to India.

From looking up at the dizzying height of the dome, when we look down, we see that the floor of the hall is paved in geometrical patterns. Eight-pointed stars and cruciform shapes

◆ *Lord Curzon's bronze lamp*

alternate, all inlaid with black into the marble. At the centre of this layout, finally at rest, lies Mumtaz Mahal's cenotaph. Shah Jahan's tomb was added later, so it is not in the geometrical centre—possibly the only element that is asymmetrical in the entire structure.

The cenotaphs of Shah Jahan and Mumtaz Mahal are surrounded by a screen. The original screen was made of pure

◆ *A part of the main hall*

gold. It was created by the goldsmith and poet, Bibadal Khan. He was the superintendent of the imperial goldsmiths. The screen had been made by him and his artisans at a cost of Rs 6,00,000. The gold screen was, however, removed soon after in 1643. It was considered too precious! The marble screen that replaced it has stood there ever since. Spectacularly carved, it is octagonal in shape and concentric to the hall.

◆ *Marble screen*

There are a number of international influences that appear in the Taj. The emperor was determined to use the best of techniques known worldwide, and thus, we see the use of pietra dura on the screens and the cenotaph. This technique originated in Florence, Italy. The inlay work in pietra dura is done with semi-precious stones. Red and yellow coloured stones were used in the Taj and

• *Pietra Dura*

as a result the final effect is that of a detailed painting. Flowers and plants cover the screens and cenotaphs, all done using the pietra dura technique.

Look closely at the cenotaph of Mumtaz Mahal, and you will see that it is a base topped by a sarcophagus. The base is decorated with pietra dura flowers, and the sarcophagus has Quranic inscriptions carved in a script called sulus. At the foot is written this, in a different script: 'The illumined grave of Arjumand Banu Begam, entitled Mumtaz Mahal, who died in the year 1040 (AD 1631).'

Shah Jahan's cenotaph is almost wholly covered in floral pietra dura work. Here, some flowers like poppies and lilies can be identified. In fact, the poppy was often used as decoration in tombs. A Turkish poet, Ahi, once wrote of poppies as flowers on tombs:

'May the clouds undo their hair, may sighs reverberate like thunder

And until the Day of Judgement may poppies burn on my tomb.'

Shah Jahan's epitaph on the cenotaph reads: 'This is the sacred grave of His Most Exalted Majesty, Dweller in Paradise, Second Lord of the Auspicious Conjunction, Shah Jahan, Padshah; may it ever be fragrant! The year 1076 (AD 1666).'

The surprises the Taj holds do not end here. For these cenotaphs are not the actual burial spots of the emperor and his queen. Just like Humayun and Akbar's tombs, these are just markers. A staircase leads down to the lower cenotaphs that are the actual burials. These graves are topped by

◆ *The cenotaphs of Mumtaz Mahal and Shah Jahan*

similar cenotaphs. The base of Mumtaz Mahal's cenotaph is mostly undecorated, and the upper part of the sarcophagus is covered with Quranic verses. On the sides are carved the ninety-nine names of Allah. Shah Jahan's cenotaph is again decorated with flowers.

And on to the Dome

The dome of the Taj Mahal adds the final layer to its extraordinary beauty. Shah Jahan's biographers described it as amrudi-shakl or guava shaped. Graceful and pure, it epitomizes everything Shah Jahan wanted the building and the complex to convey. The dome sits on a drum and between the two is a band of inlay work. At the top of the dome is an inverted lotus on

◆ *Dome and finial*

which is the finial or kalasha. The kalasha consists of three bulbs topped by a crescent.

The terrace, on which the dome sits, has four chhatris at the corners. Each of these is topped by domes and the chhatris themselves sit on octagonal red-sandstone plinths.

The Slanting Minarets

◆ *Minarets*

Another striking feature of the Taj Mahal are the four minarets that stand at the four corners of the platform on which the mausoleum sits. These minarets tilt outwards. Why was this done? There are many theories. Perhaps it was to avoid damage to the main monument in case they collapsed.

And yet, if you look at them from the great gate, they appear straight! The tilt provides an optical effect and corrects the perspective, so at first glance they appear perpendicular.

Minarets were used in mosques in Ottoman architecture and first appeared among the Mughals at Akbar's tomb in Sikandra. There they are located on the gate. Noor Jahan's father, Itmad-ud-Daulah's tomb, also has four minarets at four corners.

The four minarets in the Taj Mahal have tapering, cylindrical shafts rising from octagonal bases. Three circular balconies appear on these and at the top of the shafts are chhatris with finial kalashas. The shafts are covered with curved white marble blocks joined with black stone. Inside each minaret is a staircase made of sandstone. These are no longer accessible to the public. The staircases open on to the balconies through doors. The balconies have low railings that rest on brackets which have carved buds. Each balcony has a ring of inlaid band with floral patterns, as in the main structure.

And More Domes

There is a mosque on the west and the mihman khana or assembly hall on the east of the riverside terrace. These buildings complete the entire composition and provide balance and harmony to the view. The mosque is a rectangular structure topped by three domes. The mihman khana is a symmetrical structure on the eastern end.

The domes of these two structures are interesting. They sit on four arches and four squinches.

◆ *Mosque*

Have you wondered how a circular dome sits on top of a square structure? This is the question architects had to wrestle with when trying to figure out how to build domes. Ancient architects came up with two solutions that came to be known as pendentives and squinches.

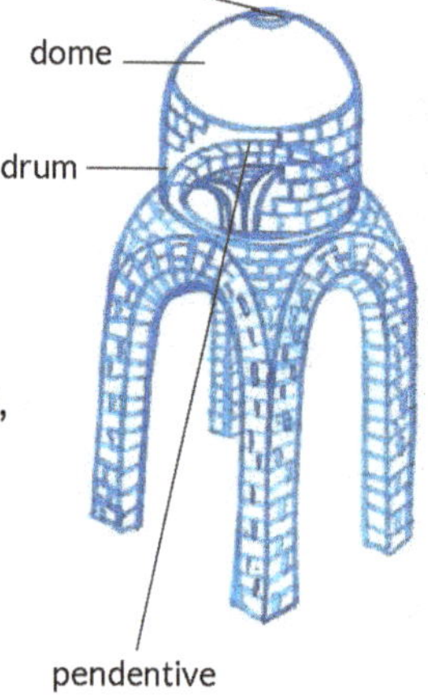

A **squinch** is a wedge that fits on the top corners of a square space. At the point where the dome's bottom edge meets the room's upper horizontal edges, four triangular-like wedges (often similar to a small bridge or arch) are placed in the corners. It is one way of getting a circular or octagonal dome to rest on a square.

A **pendentive** also supports a dome but it is more complicated, using geometry to create a series of curving and arched supports. Essentially, a pendentive is a spherical triangle that serves as an arch. Architects used four pendentives on the upper corners of a room, where they arched inward to meet the dome's circular base.

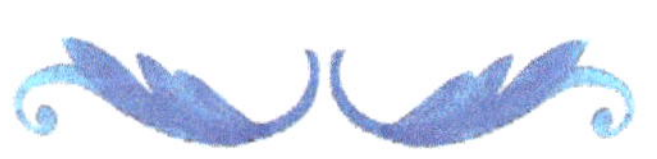

• *Pendentive*

• *Squinch*

The domes at the mihman khana have blind arches on a grid and the squinches have a pattern called muqarnas.

Muqarnas were a feature of Islamic architecture where a part of the dome—usually the area between the wall and the dome—had a three-dimensional honeycombed pattern. Muqarnas are also called stalactite vaults.

• *Muqarnas*

Standing in Taj Ganj

Imagine you have travelled back three hundred years. You stood at the jilaukhana and saw the most breathtaking sight in the world as you gazed at the Emperor of Hindustan's magnificent creation. But now you are hungry and tired and it is time to explore the bazaar that sits to the south of the jilaukhana. A bustling commercial centre of the city, here there are merchants selling their wares, large inns called caravanserais full of travellers, and homes of rich merchants. The writer Kalim described the place such: 'The streets of its bazaars are heart-cheering, craftsmen are engaged every day in the business of pleasure...'

This bazaar is called Taj Ganj and at one time was called Mumtazabad. The original layout of the bazaar had a central court or chauk with eight sides. The north-south axis of the Taj complex passed through this chauk. Four gates opened into the chauk. These gates, made of brick and plaster, were rectangular frames with a central arch each.

Today, this area does not retain its original formal layout. Being a bazaar, it slowly changed and is now a higgledy-piggledy network of modern and old constructions. It has been taken over by the people of Agra and is now a part of their daily lives. Some structures like the gates continue to be looked after as heritage, though.

Beauty and Perfection

And so we finish our walk around the Taj Mahal. Poets have

described its pristine beauty, travellers have swooned when they laid their eyes on it, kings and emperors and presidents and ordinary men, women and children have gazed at it and wondered at our capacity to create beauty.

The Taj is replete with symbols—from its plan, to every element in its construction and design, and even in the materials used. The main structures have red sandstone and white marble. The Mughals used both these materials in varying degrees over the years. Red sandstone was preferred as red was an imperial colour amongst the Mughals. White, on the other hand, denoted purity and spirituality. In the Taj Mahal, not only have both these been used, but there is a clear thought behind *how* they have been used. There is a clear hierarchical manner in this. The main mausoleum is entirely clad in marble, signifying that it is the most important building in the complex, and the spiritual centre. The surrounding structures and gates have a combination of the two main building materials.

Mumtaz Mahal's resting place was meant to represent her house in Paradise. In the Quran, Paradise is said to be filled with flowers and water bodies and gardens. We see all of this in the Taj Mahal. There is the meticulously designed garden with its many trees and flowering plants. And then there are the floral decorations on the buildings. These flowers carved by unknown hands into the marble and sandstones are permanent, never to perish. While the peripheral buildings have few of them, within the mausoleum, on the plinth of the riverside terrace and inside the tomb chambers there is detailed floral carvings and inlay work. All of these signify that Paradise is where Mumtaz Mahal was finally laid to rest.

But with the Taj we soon learn that there is not just one layer of meaning. There is usually yet another hidden meaning that we can find if we look some more. The flowers and flowering plants also signify Shah Jahan's rule as a great emperor. They were part of his political propaganda! His biographers wrote, probably on the direction of the emperor himself, that his rule symbolized a period of prosperity, beauty and perfection, all of which were represented through floral motifs. In the words of historians of the time, Shah Jahan was 'the spring of the flower garden of justice and generosity', and his court was the 'adornment of the meadow of pomp'. Similarly, there are several references to the imperial family, comparing them with flowers.

And this is how, the Taj Mahal, with every inch of its structure, proclaims so much—the love of a man for his wife, an earthly reflection of Paradise, a serene and spectacular final resting place, and finally, the grandeur and ambition of a great Mughal.

Who Really Built Taj Mahal?

We have walked around the Taj Mahal complex and looked at the building and the grounds in detail. Isn't it fascinating to know that this perfectly designed memorial was handcrafted by craftsmen from different parts of the country? Who were these people who built the Taj Mahal? What do we know about them?

There are no formal records or names of the craftsmen who worked to build the Taj Mahal. Craftsmen came from all over the country. It's mentioned in some accounts that twenty thousand men worked on the tomb for twenty-two years.

The Taj had skilled craftsmen of different types working on it. Stonemasons and bricklayers built the main structures. From some etchings on the walls and buildings, it seems that these people were both Hindu and Muslim. Stonecarvers spent hours and days carving out the beautiful flowering plants and mouldings that decorate the entire complex. They mostly used hammers and chisels and painstakingly carved on the stone. You can imagine the sights and sounds at the time of people talking in various languages amongst themselves as they tapped away at the stone.

While walking around the building, if you look carefully, you will find some small symbols carved into the red sandstone. These are unrelated to the decorative carvings and look like random markings.

These are guild marks or mason marks of groups of craftsmen who left these marks on the stones. Upto four hundred and twenty-five such marks have been found at various places in the complex. There are no such marks on the marble.

A Work of Many Hands

Workmen from different parts of the country and West Asia came to Agra to build the Taj Mahal. Amaanat Khan was a famous calligraphist who inscribed the passages of the Quran on the main pishtaq and gateways. The master mason was Muhammed Hanif from Baghdad, who was paid a salary of Rs 1000 a month. Amaanat Khan was paid a similar salary. Ismail Khan Rumi was the builder of the two-shell dome. But strangely, despite him having built one of the finest domes in the world, his salary was only half the amount of Hanif. Was pay scale linked to nobility? Were the others noblemen and the Turkish Rumi a commoner? We don't really know.

The inlay work where one stone would be carved out and the hollow filled with another stone of a different colour was done by parchinkars or stone inlay workers. While this kind of inlay work was prevalent for many centuries in India, the Mughals introduced the intensely skillful art of pietra dura. This craft originated in Florence in Italy. The Mughals knew of this from artists who worked in their courts and from gifts received from European visitors. Records show that the inlay workers were from Kannauj and were all Hindus. The immaculately detailed inlay work at the Taj Mahal was probably a combination of ancient Hindu craft and Italian pietra dura—together creating magic that was purely Mughal in style and execution.

Shah Jahan had a keen interest in gemology and this extended to developing the art of pietra dura in his buildings to a level of perfection. The intricate stone inlay with different gems used

◆ *Pietra dura*

in the same panel, each piece flawlessly set in a way that no joints were visible between the gems. Shah Jahan's court poet Kalim wrote, 'The inlayer has set stone on stone so [that even] the dark spot of the heart of the lala [poppy, tulip] is without joints or fissures.' The inlay work in the Taj Mahal had stones like lapis lazuli from Afghanistan, jade from Burma, sapphire from Ceylon, turquoise from Tibet. There are twenty-eight types of stones used in the parchinkari at the Taj.

When we look at the Taj Mahal it looks like it was made to perfection by divine hands. But in reality, it was crafted by the hands of hardworking men from the villages and towns of India.

They Came from Near and Far

The main materials used in the Taj Mahal are bricks, red sandstone, white marble and plaster. The bricks were burnt in kilns around Agra and were of standardized sizes. These were called lakhauri bricks. The sandstone came from Fatehpur Sikri, 40 kms from Agra. The white marble came from Makrana in Rajasthan. The stones were transported in large blocks, on carts drawn by bullocks.

The plaster that was used to finish surfaces had ingredients like lime, shells, marble dust, gum of trees like neem and babul, egg white and sugar with bael juice. The mixture was applied to the brick walls and then polished with shells and chalk powder to a brilliant shine. All this work was done by hand by skilled craftsmen. Mughal plasterwork was considered superior to that of any Western technique. A Dutch trader wrote, 'They polish it steadily with agates, perhaps for a whole day, until it is dry and hard, and shines like alabaster, or can even be used as a looking glass.'

There are no architectural drawings available of the Taj Mahal. It's deduced from various accounts, that the chief architects or supervisors would mark out the plan of the buildings on the ground to actual measurements. Based on these markings, diggers or beldars would dig the foundations.

How was the actual construction of such a massive structure done? Today, a project like this would have hundreds of engineers, architects and project managers sitting in offices and at the site, directing the process. In the 17th century, Shah Jahan's team of a few designers and master craftsmen and supervisors carried out the task.

Building a Wonder of the World

Building a strong foundation for the Taj Mahal was a challenge due to the sandy riverbanks that made the ground unstable. The court poet Kalim wrote in detail how this was addressed.

Wells made of wood were made and sunk into the sand. After that the sand that lay inside the well was removed to a depth where stable earth appeared. This cavity would then be filled with stone and rubble till the surface. This was repeated every 3.76 metres, as was discovered during excavations done in the 1950's. The plinths on this foundation were made of brick and mortar. The wood for the foundation was sal, brought from forests nearby. Use of wood in the foundations

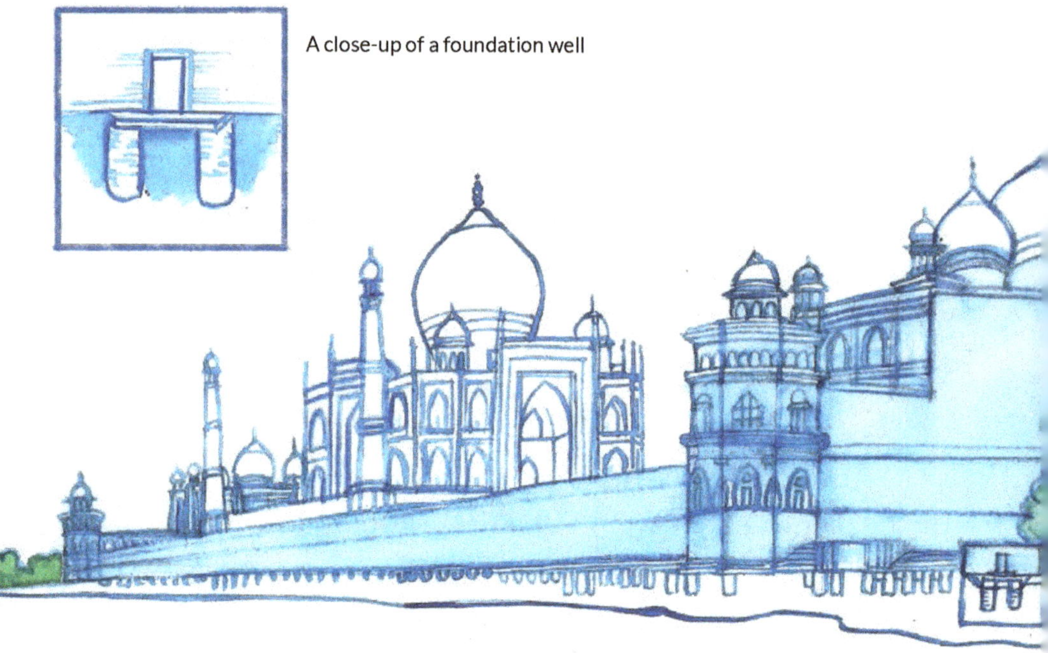

◆ Foundation wells below the Taj Mahal

indicate that the builders understood that wood was a better shock-absorber than a rigid material like masonry. This flexibility would allow the foundation to absorb shocks of any earthquakes and would limit damage to the building above.

The outer surfaces of all the domes in the complex were covered with marble. The main dome of the mausoleum was also covered in marble while all other smaller domes were covered with white plaster.

How was the material transported from their source to the site and then up to the great heights of the structures?

The white marble came from Makrana in Rajasthan which is 300 kms from Agra. Accounts written by a visitor called

Manrique Sebastian describes it. Huge slabs of marble were dragged on wagons pulled by powerful oxen and big horned buffalos. The animals were in teams of twenty or thirty and Sebastian says that despite the numbers 'they drew the sweat' of many such large teams.

As the building started progressing, materials were hoisted to the higher levels via mud ramps. Animals like oxen and elephants carried stone and masonry up these ramps, some upto 3,000 metres in length. One can imagine that the construction site would have been teeming with people and animals. A Mughal monument in construction would have been full of hustle and bustle.

As the building was constructed, a system of brick scaffolding was erected for the masons and craftsmen to reach the heights and work. It is imagined that the entire structure was enclosed within the brick scaffolding. How did the builders see the progress of the building with a layer of masonry enveloping the building? There must have been plans or models for reference. Unfortunately, there seem to be no existing records of these.

The Taj Mahal complex took twelve years to complete. After the foundations of the riverside terrace were built, work continued all over the complex. The first death anniversary of Mumtaz Mahal was held on 22 June 1632 at the construction site. By this time, the area marked for the jilaukhana was ready and this was used to set up tents and seating in rich brocades and velvet. The emperor and the gathering recited verses from the Quran. All guests were served refreshments and donations of money and food were distributed amongst the poor.

Work continued at a frenetic pace and by the following year, 1633, during the second death anniversary, the riverfront terrace and the white marble platform of the mausoleum were ready. By this time Mumtaz Mahal's body was placed in its final resting place which is at the lower level of the main platform. Urs celebrations were held on the terrace and the gold screen by Bibadal Khan was erected over the upper cenotaph that would later be the centre of the domed hall. The official recorded date of completion of construction was 1643.

Putting a Price on the Priceless

Today when we look at the Taj Mahal, a spectacularly extravagant building studded with precious stones and clad in white marble, the question arises—how much did it cost the royal treasury of those days to build this monument? Well, there are documents that have recorded that.

The cost of construction of the entire complex was Rs 50,00,000. It is calculated that twenty thousand workers were employed for various works to build the entire complex. Shah Jahan set up a waqf or an endowment of Rs 4,00,000. Revenues from the bazaars, caravanserais and the villages of Agra contributed to finance the maintenance of the Taj Mahal. This included repairs, salaries and the upkeep of the tomb attendants who lived on the premises. Later the British abolished the waqf and the maintenance of the Taj Mahal became their responsibility.

After the completion of the Taj Mahal, the Quran would be recited day and night by tomb attendants appointed by Shah Jahan. He visited the tomb and recited the fatiha himself. Several of Mumtaz Mahal's death anniversaries were celebrated with prayers and charitable donations by the emperor.

Shah Jahan's last visit to the Taj Mahal was in 1654. The noblemen accompanying him were commanded to wait outside at the jamat khana (place of gathering). The priests sat in the outer chamber. He stood alone over Mumtaz Mahal's grave and prayed for her soul.

◆ *Taj Mahal from across the river*

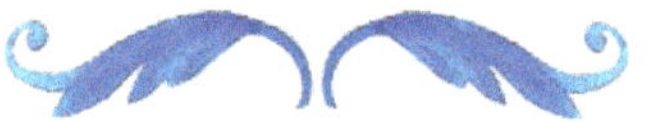

We have seen how the Taj Mahal was probably encased in a dense **brick scaffolding** as it was being built. Once the construction was completed, this scaffolding was probably removed in stages. There are stories that relate how Shah Jahan announced that the people of Agra could take the bricks of the scaffolding for free. And apparently as a result, the scaffolding was removed overnight as people took away the kiln burnt bricks to build their own homes. Can you imagine what a sight it must have been for the people of Agra when the scaffolding disappeared and the building came into view? It must have been a stunning sight for the poor and rich citizens of Agra alike—to see the shimmering dome of the Taj Mahal floating in the horizon of Agra city.

Shah Jahan survived another thirty-five years after the death of Mumtaz Mahal. Soon after the completion of the mausoleum, he moved from Agra to Delhi, to build the city of Shahjahanabad.

Towards the end of 1657, Shah Jahan fell ill, while he was still in Delhi. He had spent the last decade building Shahjahanabad. But now, with his illness slowly crippling him, he gave the charge of his administration to his eldest son Dara Shikoh and retired to his palace in the Agra Fort.

However, soon after, in a series of coups, Aurangzeb lay siege to the Agra Fort. He defeated his brothers and captured the Agra Fort, making his father a prisoner. Shah Jahan's main companion, during his years in captivity, was his eldest daughter Jahanara. He spent these years of imprisonment, possibly remembering his various successes as an emperor. The crowning glory amongst these would be the Taj Mahal.

When he died in captivity, in 1666, at the Agra Fort, his daughter Jahanara arranged for his funeral rites. He was interred with formalities by the side of the tomb of Mumtaz Mahal, in the Taj Mahal. With his death ended the life of one of the Great Mughals who would be known for centuries to come for his various achievements as an emperor. But his greatest claim in the pages of history would be as the creator of one of the most beautiful buildings on earth—the Taj Mahal.

The Legacy of the Taj Mahal

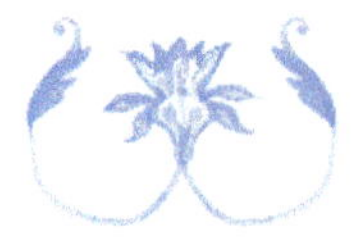

With the passing of Shah Jahan, the Taj Mahal disappeared from the accounts written by Mughal historians. Aurangzeb died in 1707 and with his death, the Mughal dynasty fell into chaos. Repeatedly attacked by the Marathas and the Jats, the empire started shrinking.

Once Mughal power declined, Agra was attacked and looted again and again. The Jat ruler, Suraj Mal, who ruled from Bharatpur was one of the plunderers of the city. Later the Marathas took over.

After centuries of prosperity, Agra slowly started decaying. At the time of the construction of the Taj Mahal, Agra had become the converging point for artisans, artists and craftsmen from all over the country. It had become a centre of artistic excellence. But as the seat of power moved north to Delhi, the glamour of the city started fading.

Enter the British

Towards the end of the 18th century, the British East India Company had extended its control over various parts of India. They set up their own representatives, called Residents, within the courts of the Marathas. One of these was Major William Palmer who was located in Agra. He stationed himself with his troops in the jilaukhana of the Taj complex. This set off a period when the grounds of the Taj Mahal became host to British officers and citizens. By 1803, Agra was in British hands after the Second Maratha War. The Taj Mahal became a tourist attraction for the British and through their accounts and descriptions, the rest of the world came to know of it.

Before the mutiny of 1857 there was a period when the Taj Mahal had become a 'pleasure resort'. Indians and British alike visited the complex in large numbers. Tents were set up in the gardens for visitors. There were occasions when the British military band played on the marble terrace and picnic parties were held in the gardens. Lavish banquets were arranged in the premises. Europeans ate and drank at the jamaat khana, the gardens were decorated with lamps, music from orchestras filled the air and guests were later entertained by fireworks set off on the riverbank. There are accounts of British officers using hammer and chisel to pick out the precious gems from the pietra dura work that decorated large areas of the main mausoleum. Drunken soldiers lay in the lawns and there is even a story of a lady falling to her death from the edge of the main terrace! It certainly was far removed from the solemn representation of Paradise that Shah Jahan had envisioned.

When the Indian Mutiny happened in 1857, Agra was looted and army barracks were set up inside the Agra Fort by the British, as they tried to quell the uprising. The East India Company gave way to the British Empire in India and the fortune of Agra also changed. From being a capital city for the Mughal royalty it became a city that was mainly a cantonment town.

As power changed hands from the Mughals to the Marathas and later to the British, the Taj Mahal stood, mostly unscathed. Well before the Mutiny of 1857, the British had set up a framework to restore the Taj Mahal. A British army officer, Captain Taylor, was appointed to repair the Taj Mahal in 1810. He apparently reported repairs of the façade where the jewels had been prised out. However, it was discovered later that these repairs were mainly done with coloured plaster. Initial surveys done at that time showed that the main building had survived without extensive damage since it was built. The peripheral buildings, however, had fallen into disrepair.

The earliest reference, soon after it was built, of any restoration work at the tomb is in a letter written by Aurangzeb to Shah Jahan in 1652. In this he writes that the dome of the mausoleum and some other areas had water leakages during the monsoon season. Repairs were carried out to fix these problems. There were no further references to these leaks once the British took over the care of the monument.

Over the years, various efforts were made towards the maintenance and preservation of the Taj Mahal by the British. Most of this was limited to repairs at the main mausoleum.

Lord Curzon took a special interest in the Taj Mahal and for the first time, restoration at the Taj Mahal complex extended to the garden and other structures. He put an end to the complex being used as an entertainment area which had earlier resulted in misuse and vandalizing of the gardens and buildings.

Curzon spent a large amount of money in the restoration. He is responsible for the current lawns of the Taj Mahal. The profusion of plants and trees that had been originally planted were thinned out to allow a better view of the main mausoleum. The cypress trees were replanted. From the garden of Paradise that Shah Jahan had created, the Taj Mahal was now an English garden. What we see today is a version of Curzon's gardens.

Parts of the jilaukhana which had fallen to disrepair were rebuilt. Several local artisans were engaged to cut marble, repair mosaics and patch cracks. The water supply system from the river was repaired and the fountains sprang into life again. The mosque and the jammat khana had needed extensive repairs, all of which were carried out. This was the time Lord Curzon ordered the brass lamp from Cairo which hangs over the cenotaphs. He considered the Taj as one of the most beautiful monuments in the world. After the completion

In 1860, the **Archaeological Survey of India (ASI)** was founded. Initially the main agenda of ASI was to record monuments. Under Lord Curzon, in 1905, this was redefined. The Ancient Monuments Preservation Act, 1904, defined that the archaeological and conservation work was to be conducted and controlled nationwide. This meant that the ASI would take care of the maintenance and protection of ancient monuments in the country.

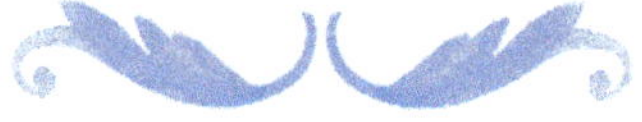

of the restoration project, he said, 'Every rupee has been an offering of reverence to the past and a gift of recovered beauty to the future.'

A Teardrop on the Cheek of Time

After the independence of India, the Indian government took over the Archaeological Survey of India (ASI) and the conservation policies for all heritage monuments in India were determined by the new government.

One of the controversies that arose around the conservation of the Taj Mahal was the construction of an oil refinery in

Mathura which is 40 kms from Agra. The refinery was commissioned in 1972 and became operational by 1983. During the time of its planning there was valid concern that chemical emissions from the refinery would affect the marble of the Taj Mahal.

In 1982, the Taj Mahal was recognized by UNESCO as a World Heritage Site. As part of its steps to protect the monument the government set up a 50 kms-radius around Agra within which no polluting industry could be set up. As awareness grew about the effect of pollution on the Taj Mahal, various measures were taken to control the environment around it.

Today, no polluting vehicles are allowed within 500 metres of the monument. No new construction is allowed within 200 metres of the Taj Mahal boundary.

But none of the measures taken to protect the Taj Mahal included the city of Agra. Today the Taj Mahal is guarded by the Central Industrial Security Force (CISF) and several steps have been taken to protect the monument from environmental decay. But the discussion on protecting the Taj Mahal has not extended to include the city of Agra. While funds from international organizations are poured into protecting the glistening white marble of the Taj, the city outside falls to disrepair.

Agra has 17 lakh residents. The number of visitors is many times more. Yet the city faces power and water shortages. While walking through the congested streets of Agra, it's common to see noisy diesel generators outside shops further polluting the air. The 'snow-fed' Yamuna, on the banks of which the city had grown in the heydays of the Mughal kings, is now a rivulet. The shortage of water in homes has led to people tapping the groundwater. This is pushing the water table down further. There is hardly any organized public transportation in Agra. It's quite common to get stuck in traffic jams anywhere in the city.

With high-speed connectivity from cities like Delhi via trains and expressways, it is now very common for tourists to visit Agra on a day-trip. Therefore, the citizens of Agra do not get any economic benefit out of the tourism industry. The visitors do not stay to explore the city beyond the walls of the Taj Mahal complex. The families living in Taj Ganj, who are descendants of the craftsmen who had built the Taj Mahal, never meet the tourists who drift in and out only to see the architectural wonder that overshadows everything in Agra.

◆ *Taj Mahal and the modern city of Agra today*

The government and conservationists have set up a buffer zone around the Taj Mahal to protect it, but the same circle of protection is isolating it from the city within which it stands. While the Taj Mahal is an international attraction, like a glamorous movie star it sits aloof, cut off from the normal everyday life around it. If this situation continues, the value of the Taj Mahal in the eyes of the locals will continue to diminish and there will be little emotional connect between the marvellous structure and its immediate neighbours.

We have read how Agra was at one time an important centre for the rulers of Hindustan. Beautiful gardens, an aesthetically developed riverfront, a river fed by Himalayan snow, bustling markets and a rich aristocracy made this city thrive. Today, efforts have to be made to bring the city back to its former glory.

Instead of merely protecting a monument, the economy of the city of Agra needs to be revived. The conservation effort has to extend to not just the building and the garden of the Taj Mahal. We have to think beyond that and plan to restore an entire culture that once thrived in Agra.

• *Contemporary craftsmen in Agra using ancient techniques in their work*

The riverfront of Agra for which it was famous, should be redeveloped. The families living in Taj Ganj, who possibly have centuries of history in their homes that link them to the building of Agra and the Taj Mahal, can be included in the tourist tapestry of Agra. It would be delightful to wander the alleys of Taj Ganj and listen to stories from these families

of their forefathers building the Taj Mahal. Making the population of Agra a part of the Taj story would benefit them economically and also reconnect them with their cultural heritage.

The Taj Mahal was built as a paradisical resting place for Mumtaz Mahal. A place of utmost piety, the Quranic verses that decorate the building and the cenotaphs have wrapped the place with a purity that is reflected in the perfectly balanced architectural plan and the pristine white marble that encases the structure. Shah Jahan had created the Taj Mahal like a piece of precious jewel, perfect in every way. But he was also

The poet **Rabindranath Tagore** wrote
of Shah Jahan and the Taj Mahal:

'Though emeralds, rubies, pearls are all
But as the glitter of a rainbow tricking our empty air
And must pass away,

Yet still one solitary tear
Would hang on the cheek of time
In the form
Of this white and gleaming Taj Mahal.'

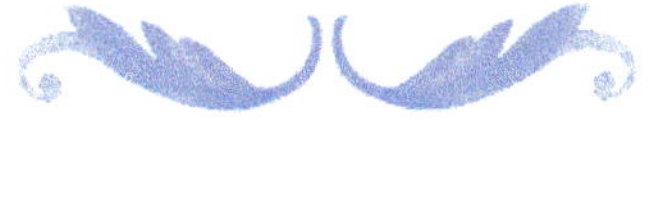

an emperor who built to leave behind an everlasting legacy that the world would admire. The Taj Mahal is as much a resting place for an empress and an emperor as it is a wonder of the world that plays host to people from every corner of the country and the world.

This architectural marvel and its story need to be preserved for posterity. Only then, in the centuries to come, people will see it in the changing light of the day and night and imagine how twenty thousand craftsmen and a king got together to build one of the most beautiful buildings in the world.

Author's Note

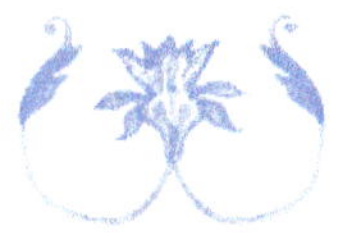

Have you wondered how these fantastic monuments are built so perfectly—symmetrical, every side of the building meeting at perfect corners, not a window out of place? That is because most buildings start as drawings on paper (and now on the computer using design software).

There are three basic drawings that architects make to explain the design to the construction team. These are called Plan, Elevation and Section.

Together, they represent a building graphically. These drawings are two-dimensional representations of the building—as if the building was a flat object. In this way, a whole room or building can be shown on one piece of paper. To fit the whole building on paper, the drawing must be drawn to a scale. That means 1 centimetre on the paper might represent 100 centimetres in the real world.

A **plan** is a drawing of a building as seen from top—like a bird's eye view. Imagine taking the roof off a building and looking down inside it. What you see is what an architect calls the floor plan. It shows the layout of a building with all the dimensions marked out. It is the main drawing that is used

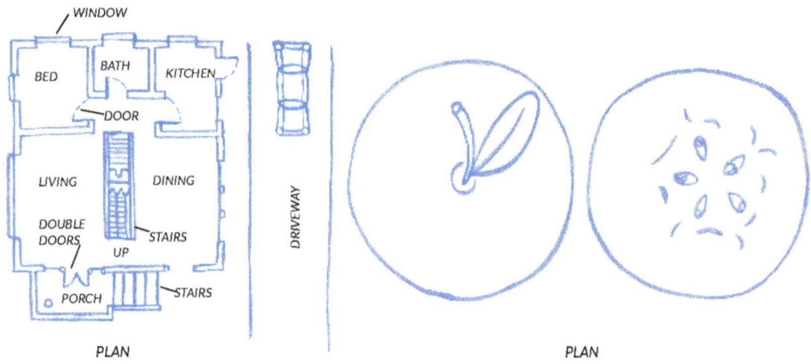

when construction starts.

An **elevation** is a drawing of a building as seen from one side. It could be the front or side of the building. It gives the viewer an idea of some key features of the building such as height, length, width and external appearance. Architects use

elevations to study the external appearance of a building.

Section drawings give a more complete idea of what a building might look like when it is built. They are drawn from a vertical plane slicing through a building, as if you sliced from top to bottom and stood looking straight at it. It is used to show the heights and vertical measurements. These drawings allow us to see the features inside a building.

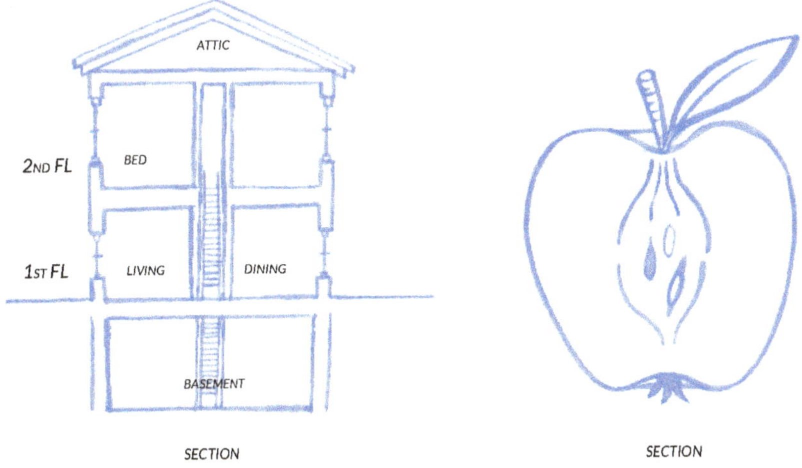

Acknowledgements

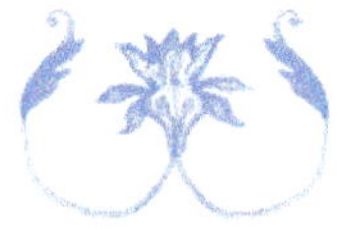

The idea of doing a series of books that bring together history and architecture and tell the stories of monuments that give children a glimpse into our rich design heritage was something I had long wanted to do. I have often lamented the abysmal lack of design orientation in the Indian education curriculum and I feel that this leads directly to a population that is aloof to heritage and conservation and a landscape that is mostly insensitive to good design. Our cities are growing rapidly but are they architecturally evolved or forward-thinking? We need to develop an innate sense of appreciation of the arts and equally an awareness of how that was dealt with historically.

This series that tells the story of some stunning Indian monuments intends to be a step in that direction, with the hope that children will appreciate and understand the world of architecture and how it has evolved.

I spent many delightful hours researching the Taj Mahal. Amita Baig of World Monuments Fund shared many invaluable thoughts on the city of Agra, its growth and how Shah Jahan's vision may have evolved around the Taj. Her book, *Taj Mahal: Multiple Narratives* co-authored with Rahul Mehrotra, was a detailed study of the process of planning, design and execution by Shah Jahan and his team of master craftsmen.

Swapna Liddle, historian, writer and of Intach Delhi Chapter, was brilliant with her insights on the structure of the book. The late children's writer Subhadra Sen Gupta chatted with me over coffee, telling me how she writes history for children. I wish she could have seen this book and reviewed it.

I read *A Teardrop on the Cheek of Time* by Diana Preston and Michael Preston overnight, trailing Babur, Humayun, Akbar, Jahangir and Shah Jahan as the Mughal Empire grew and grew more. Giles Tillotson's *Taj Mahal* was an excellent insight into the Taj Mahal's structure and history.

The Complete Taj Mahal by Ebba Koch was an eye-opener to every structure that was built in the Taj Mahal complex. Its exhaustive studies of plans and details were invaluable for me to study and glean from. Amita Baig loaned me her much marked copy of *Taj Mahal, The Illumined Tomb – An Anthology of Seventeenth-Century Mughal and European Documentary Sources*, by W. E. Begley and Z. A. Desai. I thoroughly enjoyed reading through Mughal documents and resources in this title. The Taj Mahal was well-documented when built and this book is a ready reckoner for anyone looking for support to quash current controversies on the structure's antecedents. Philip Davies' *Monuments of India, Volume 2* was a perfect overview of the Islamic, Rajput and European era in India and I keep going back to its pages for references.

Warm gratitude to my dear friend Vikas Chhabra for some stunning photographs of the Taj Mahal and Sikandra.

The Mughal queens and kings are astonishingly colourful, each one of them worth reading more about. I have made passing references to the characters of Babur, Humayun, Akbar, Noor Jahan and the rest of the cast but I would encourage all readers of this book to find more stories about them. They are fascinating and as interesting as any fictional characters. Their lives were full of drama and tragedy and fanfare. Fairy tales would be put to shade by the stories of the Mughal royalty and their households. I hope this book gives a foretaste to that delicious and rich set of legends to the reader.

Finally, this series and this book would not have been produced without the thought bubbles that emanate from the fertile mind of Ravi Singh, Publisher, Speaking Tiger and his most able 'mantri' Sudeshna Shome Ghosh, Publisher of Talking Cub. Ravi's idea became a reality with Sudeshna's patience with my manuscript. The book is designed beautifully by Maithili Doshi who dealt with my briefs for illustrations and photographs without a grumble. The sketches are lovely and am so grateful to Kavita Singh Kale for drawing them out with the greatest care.

I hope this book inspires its readers to know more of our history, the stories of the past and apply that to their futures, taking care to build environments that are worth writing books about.

Picture Credits

Page 19, Humayun's Tomb, Junaid Ahmad Ansari, Unsplash

Page 26, Shah Jahan on the Peacock Throne, Wikimedia Commons

Page 28, Shah Jahan and Mumtaz Mahal, Wikimedia Commons

Page 34, Ahukhna in Burhanpur, Madhya Pradesh, Wikimedia Commons, Yashasvi Nagda

Page 39, Shalimar Bagh, Wikimedia Commons, Pradeep K. Joshi

Page 47, An example of a chhatri, Wikimedia Commons, Arooj-un-Nisa

Page 52, Taj Mahal, Unsplash, Sanin

Page 58, The arcades of the jilaukhana, Unsplash

Page 59, The modern city of Agra comes up to the gates of the Taj, Vikas Chhabra

Page 62, View of Taj from Mehtab Garden, Wikimedia Commons, LittleDwangs

Page 64-65, A view of the gardens from the Taj Mahal, Wikimedia Commons

Page 66, Main entrance to the Taj Mahal, Wikimedia Commons, Rajesnewdelhi

Page 67, Details of the main entrance, Wikimedia Commons

Page 69, Garden-wall pavilions, or Naubat Khana, Wikimedia Commons, Biswarup Ganguly

Page 72, The Taj Mahal with the mosque and Naubat Khana, Wikimedia Commons, Antrix3

Page 73, The trees around the Taj today, Vikas Chhabra

Page 74, Taj Mahal, Vikas Chhabra

Page 75, Blind arches, Wikimedia Commons

Page 81, The floral patterns and calligraphy at the entrance, Wikimedia Commons

Page 83, Lord Curzon's bronze lamp, Wikimedia Commons

Page 84, A part of the main hall

Page 84, Marble screen, Wikimedia Commons, https://wellcomeimages. org/indexplus/obf_images/db/2e/d60bfc71bf00501db711d6fcddfb.jpg

Page 85, Pietra dura, Wikimedia Commons

Page 86, Cenotaphs, Wikimedia Commons

Page 87, Dome and finial, Wikimedia Commons

Page 88, Minarets, Wikimedia Commons

Page 89, Mosque, Wikimedia Commons

Page 91, Pedentive, Wikimedia Commons, Varun Shiv Kapoor

Page 91, Squinch, Vikas Chhabra

Page 91, Muqarna, Wikimedia Commons, Fulvio

Page 97, Pietra dura, Vikas Chhabra

Page 103, Taj Mahal from across the river, Wikimedia Commons

Page 112, Taj Mahal and the city of Agra today, Wikimedia Commons, Ryan

Page 113, Contemporary craftsmen using ancient techniques in Agra, Wikimedia Commons

Page 114, South Gate of the Taj Mahal opening in from Taj Ganj, Wikimedia Commons, Divya Gupta

Illustration references for page 42-43, 57, 58-59

The Complete Taj Mahal, Bookwise (India) Pvt, Ltd, 2006

~ Magnificent Monuments of India ~
The Kailash Temple at Ellora
How Art was Etched in Stone

By Tilottama Shome
Illustrated by Kavita Singh Kale

Go on a journey right back into the time of gods and demons, kings and queens and when an awe-inspiring work of art was brought to life on stone.

The Kailash Temple at Ellora is considered to be a pinnacle of ancient Indian art, architecture and sculpture. Built by Rashtrakuta king Krishna I in the eighth century CE, the temple is part of the Ellora Cave complex near Aurangabad in Maharashtra. Carved out of rock from the hills, the temple is dedicated to Shiva and is a wonder of ancient architecture and construction techniques.

In this book, which is filled with photographs and illustrations, Tilottama Shome explains concepts of Hindu temple architecture, narrates tales from history, folklore and mythology, and brings to life this magnificent example of art and architecture for a young reader.